EFFECTIVE ASSESSMENT
FOR STUDENTS
WITH
SPECIAL NEEDS

A PRACTICAL APPROACH TO SPECIAL EDUCATION FOR EVERY TEACHER

The Fundamentals of Special Education
A Practical Guide for Every Teacher

The Legal Foundations of Special Education
A Practical Guide for Every Teacher

Effective Assessment for Students With Special Needs
A Practical Guide for Every Teacher

Effective Instruction for Students With Special Needs
A Practical Guide for Every Teacher

*Working With Families and Community Agencies to
    Support Students With Special Needs*
A Practical Guide for Every Teacher

Public Policy, School Reform, and Special Education
A Practical Guide for Every Teacher

Teaching Students With Sensory Disabilities
A Practical Guide for Every Teacher

Teaching Students With Medical, Physical, and Multiple Disabilities
A Practical Guide for Every Teacher

Teaching Students With Learning Disabilities
A Practical Guide for Every Teacher

Teaching Students With Communication Disorders
A Practical Guide for Every Teacher

Teaching Students With Emotional Disturbance
A Practical Guide for Every Teacher

Teaching Students With Mental Retardation
A Practical Guide for Every Teacher

Teaching Students With Gifts and Talents
A Practical Guide for Every Teacher

EFFECTIVE ASSESSMENT
FOR STUDENTS
WITH
SPECIAL NEEDS

A Practical Guide for Every Teacher

JIM YSSELDYKE
BOB ALGOZZINE

CORWIN PRESS
A SAGE Publications Company
Thousand Oaks, California

For information:

Corwin Press
A Sage Publications Company
2455 Teller Road
Thousand Oaks, California 91320
www.corwinpress.com

Sage Publications Ltd.
1 Oliver's Yard
55 City Road
London EC1Y 1SP
United Kingdom

Sage Publications India Pvt. Ltd.
B-42, Panchsheel Enclave
Post Box 4109
New Delhi 110 017 India

Printed in the United States of America

Library of Congress Cataloging-in-Publication Data

Ysseldyke, James E.
Effective assessment for students with special needs: A practical guide for every teacher / James E. Ysseldyke & Bob Algozzine.
    p. cm.
Includes bibliographical references and index.
ISBN 1-4129-3943-7 (cloth)
ISBN 1-4129-3896-1 (pbk.)
    1. Exceptional children—Ability testing—United States. 2. Special education teachers—Training of—United States. 3. Special education—United States.
I. Algozzine, Robert. II. Title.
LC3981.Y873 2006
371.904

                                                        2005037819

This book is printed on acid-free paper.

06   07   08   09   10   9   8   7   6   5   4   3   2   1

Acquisitions Editor:	Kylee M. Liegl
Editorial Assistant:	Nadia Kashper
Production Editor:	Denise Santoyo
Copy Editor:	Colleen Brennan
Typesetter:	C&M Digitals (P) Ltd.
Indexer:	Kathy Paparchontis
Cover Designer:	Michael Dubowe

Contents

About
A Practical Approach to Special Education for Every Teacher

*S*pecial education means specially designed instruction for students with unique learning needs. Students receive special education for many reasons. Students with disabilities such as mental retardation, hearing impairments (including deafness), speech or language impairments, visual impairments (including blindness), emotional disturbance, orthopedic impairments, autism, traumatic brain injury, other health impairments, or specific learning disabilities are entitled to special education services. Students who are gifted and talented also receive special education. Special education services are delivered in many settings, including regular classes, resource rooms, and separate classes. The 13 books of this collection will help you teach students with disabilities and those with gifts and talents. Each book focuses on a specific area of special education and can be used individually or in conjunction with all or some of the other books. Six of the books provide the background and content knowledge you need in order to work effectively with all students with unique learning needs:

Book 1: The Fundamentals of Special Education

Book 2: The Legal Foundations of Special Education

Book 3: Effective Assessment for Students With Special Needs

Book 4: Effective Instruction for Students With Special Needs

Book 5: Working With Families and Community Agencies to Support Students With Special Needs

Book 6: Public Policy, School Reform, and Special Education

Seven of the books focus on teaching specific groups of students who receive special education:

Book 7:   Teaching Students With Sensory Disabilities

Book 8:   Teaching Students With Medical, Physical, and Multiple Disabilities

Book 9:   Teaching Students With Learning Disabilities

Book 10: Teaching Students With Communication Disorders

Book 11: Teaching Students With Emotional Disturbance

Book 12: Teaching Students With Mental Retardation

Book 13: Teaching Students With Gifts and Talents

All of the books in *A Practical Approach to Special Education for Every Teacher* will help you to make a difference in the lives of all students, especially those with unique learning needs.

ACKNOWLEDGMENTS

The approach we take in *A Practical Approach to Special Education for Every Teacher* is an effort to change how professionals learn about special education. The 13 separate books are a result of prodding from our students and from professionals in the field to provide a set of materials that "cut to the chase" in teaching them about students with disabilities and about building the capacity of systems to meet those students' needs. Teachers told us that in their classes they always confront students with special learning needs and students their school district has assigned a label to (e.g., students with learning disabilities). Our students and the professionals we worked with wanted a very practical set of texts that gave them the necessary **information** *about* **the students** (e.g., federal definitions, student characteristics) and specific **information on** *what to do about* **the students** (assessment and teaching strategies, approaches that work). They also wanted the opportunity to purchase parts of textbooks, rather than entire texts, to learn what they needed.

The production of this collection would not have been possible without the support and assistance of many colleagues. Professionals associated with Corwin Press—Faye Zucker, Kylee Liegl, Robb Clouse—helped us work through the idea of introducing special education differently, and their support in helping us do it is deeply appreciated.

Faye Ysseldyke and Kate Algozzine, our children, and our grandchildren also deserve recognition. They have made the problems associated with the project very easy to diminish, deal with, or dismiss. Every day in every way, they enrich our lives and make us better. We are grateful for them.

About the Authors

Jim Ysseldyke, PhD, is Birkmaier Professor in the Department of Educational Psychology, director of the School Psychology Program, and director of the Center for Reading Research at the University of Minnesota. Widely requested as a staff developer and conference speaker, he brings more than 30 years of research and teaching experience to educational professionals around the globe.

As the former director of the federally funded National Center on Educational Outcomes, Ysseldyke conducted research and provided technical support that helped to boost the academic performance of students with disabilities and improve school assessment techniques nationally. Today he continues to work to improve the education of students with disabilities.

The author of more than 300 publications on special education and school psychology, Ysseldyke is best known for his textbooks on assessment, effective instruction, issues in special education, and other cutting-edge areas of education and school psychology. With *A Practical Approach to Special Education for Every Teacher,* he seeks to equip educators with practical knowledge and methods that will help them to better engage students in exploring—and meeting—all their potentials.

Bob Algozzine, PhD, is professor in the Department of Educational Leadership at the University of North Carolina at Charlotte and project codirector of the U.S. Department of Education–supported Behavior and Reading Improvement Center. With 25 years of research experience and extensive first-hand knowledge of teaching students classified as seriously emotionally disturbed (and other equally useless terms),

Algozzine is a uniquely qualified staff developer, conference speaker, and teacher of behavior management and effective teaching courses.

As an active partner and collaborator with professionals in the Charlotte-Mecklenburg schools in North Carolina and as an editor of several journals focused on special education, Algozzine keeps his finger on the pulse of current special education practice. He has written more than 250 manuscripts on special education topics, authoring many popular books and textbooks on how to manage emotional and social behavior problems. Through *A Practical Approach to Special Education for Every Teacher,* Algozzine hopes to continue to help improve the lives of students with special needs—and the professionals who teach them.

Self-Assessment 1

Before you begin this book, check your knowledge and understanding of the content being covered. Choose the best answer for each of the following questions.

1. _____ is not a way to gather data on students.

    a. Record review

    b. Observation

    c. Interviewing

    d. Revelation

2. The process of collecting data to decide whether more intensive assessment is needed is called:

    a. Referral

    b. Screening

    c. Program evaluation

    d. Eligibility determination

3. The process of breaking complex student work into component skills is called:

    a. Task analysis

    b. Portfolio assessment

    c. Ecobehavioral assessment

    d. Performance assessment

4. When one assesses those skills necessary to perform successfully in a setting (e.g., college) we call this:

   a. Portfolio assessment

   b. Environmental appraisal

   c. Job analysis

   d. Inference

5. Scores that are significantly above or below average are called:

   a. Scaled scores

   b. Normal curve equivalents

   c. Discrepant scores

   d. Percentiles

6. Tests that measure skills in academic content areas are called:

   a. Content assessments

   b. Achievement tests

   c. Diagnostic tests

   d. Personality tests

7. _____ is the measurement term used to refer to consistency in measurement.

   a. Validity

   b. Reliability

   c. Representativeness

   d. Correlation

8. Assessment is:

   a. Testing students to determine their strengths and weaknesses

   b. A process of collecting data for the purpose of making decisions

   c. Always tailored to the individual

   d. Testing used to decide who is eligible for special education

9. When a test is modified to provide a more appropriate picture of a person with a specific disability, this is called:

   a. Accommodation

   b. Flexibility

   c. Accountability

   d. Alternate assessment

10. Which is true?

   a. Assessment is a way to test.

   b. Assessment should be directed at improving instruction.

   c. Students who perform poorly on tests are eligible for special education services.

   d. Students who are disadvantaged perform poorly on tests.

REFLECTION

1. Throughout this book we will refer to formal and informal assessment procedures and to structured and unstructured procedures. For example, we will talk about informal assessment, structured interviews, unstructured

interviews, and formal assessment. Distinguish between formal and informal approaches, and between structured and unstructured approaches.

2. Identify four kinds of behaviors sampled by intelligence tests, and say how they are different.

3. We will identify several assumptions about the skills of those who give tests. Name four. What is the effect of violating the assumptions?

4. *Acculturation* is a term used to describe an individual's background of experiences and knowledge. Why is it important that those who assess students take acculturation into account? How does acculturation affect test performance? What happens if an examiner fails to consider a student's acculturation when making assessment decisions?

Introduction to Effective Assessment for Students With Special Needs

Eleanor is not allowed to enter school because her performance on a test indicates that she is not yet "ready." **Heidi** is told to repeat second grade because her performance on a set of tests indicates she has not yet mastered second-grade content. **José** is assigned to a class for students who are gifted, while **Zeke** is placed in a class for students with learning disabilities. These placements were dependent on how the students performed on a set of tests. **Ariel** is admitted to Florida State University, but **Clem** is denied admission because his test scores are too low. **Mark**, an all-city basketball player, cannot attend a Division 1 college because his scores on the SAT are too low, even though his grades are high enough. **Randy** gets a scholarship because of his very high test scores. **Kate** earns a high score on a selection test and gets a position with General Mills; **Esther** does not do well on the test and isn't offered a position. **Manuel** wants to be a policeman, but the score he earned on the police exam places him 286th in line for hiring. This year, the city expects to hire 21 police officers.

For all of these young people, and others like them, testing can have a major effect on life choices and opportunities. American schools and society place considerable emphasis on test results. We estimate that the nation's more than 50 million elementary and secondary students take 150 million separate tests annually as part of the standardized testing mandated by states and school districts. An additional 150 million tests are given to students over and above state or district requirements. American school children take more tests than other children in the world. And, with new federal mandates to test all students in Grades 3 through 8 every year, the numbers will increase.

Testing plays a major role in **assessment**, the process by which teachers and other school personnel collect information to make decisions about students. Historically in special and remedial education, and now increasingly in general education as well, the focus of assessment has been on student progress toward instructional goals and on the extent to which students need special education and related services. In addition to testing, educators gather data by:

Observing students' behaviors

Interviewing students or those who work with them

Reviewing work samples

For students who are exceptional, assessment is especially critical because it helps educators decide whether they should receive special education services, what the specific nature of their instruction should be, and the extent to which they are making educational progress.

In this book, we look at the ways assessment data are used to make decisions about students with disabilities and those who are gifted and talented, the ways in which information is obtained, and the particular type of information collected from various assessment activities. We also discuss standards for conducting assessment and some guidelines for best practice.

1

What Should Every Teacher Know About Assessment for Decision-Making Purposes?

The process of assessing students' special educational needs usually begins when a teacher or parent recognizes a need. Because of the complex system that has evolved in delivering special education services, students must be assessed before they are eligible for services. Students who are exceptional also are assessed as part of their daily educational programs, to determine what they already know and to keep track of their progress (Taylor, 2002). Assessment is therefore a part of each phase of the special education process. The decisions that are made using assessment information are listed in *Table 1.1.* Each of the 12 areas are discussed in the following sections.

SCREENING DECISIONS

Screening is the process of collecting data to decide whether more intensive assessment is necessary. School personnel have

Table 1.1   Decisions Made Using Assessment Information

Screening decisions

Special help or enrichment

Referrals to intervention assistance teams

Intervention assistance

Referrals for psychoeducational evaluation

Exceptionality decisions

Special learning needs

Eligibility or entitlement

Instructional planning

Progress evaluation

Program evaluation

Accountability

neither the time nor the resources to test all students to find if they have special needs; instead they screen them.

Early Screening

Screening takes place at all levels of education. Children are screened before they enter kindergarten or first grade to determine their readiness in language, cognitive and motor development, and in social and emotional functioning. They may also be given vision and hearing tests. Once screened, a child's performance is compared to standards established by those who develop the screening tests. For example, if two-thirds of the children who took the test when it was being developed scored 300 points or better, children who score below 300 may be considered "at risk."

Test developers usually provide cutoff scores to help educators make decisions. These scores, called **norms**, are based on the performance of those who took the test during its development. Formal statistical standards for normality and abnormality may be used, or standards may be set by a state department of education or school district.

Some students are denied school entrance if they score below a cutoff score on a screening test. (Parents are asked to hold the child back until he or she is ready to enter school.) Sometimes low scores also result in observing and monitoring the child's performance over time.

Later Screening

Screening is used throughout the school years to identify students who need extra help because their performance or progress is markedly different from "normal" or "average." Cutoff scores for this type of screening are based on the average performance of students of similar ages or grade levels. The scores of the norm group are used to decide whether or not more testing is necessary.

Screening may also be accomplished by gathering data on student performance and progress using a set of procedures that are a part of problem-solving models or Response to Intervention models. When students are shown to be performing poorly relative to their peers or when they do not make progress at the same rate as others in their class, then they are considered at risk and specific changes are made in their instructional program.

When a student's score indicates a special need, he or she may be referred for **psychoeducational assessment** (individually administered psychological and educational tests). These tests determine the specific reasons for a student's performance on a screening measure. Usually they are administered by school psychologists or other professionals working for the school district or by service providers (e.g., private clinics, hospitals).

Implicit in screening is the notion that students' difficulties may go unnoticed or worsen if not checked. For example, a student might have a hearing difficulty that interferes with her school performance. Without screening, this difficulty may not be recognized and may not be addressed, leading to continued low performance.

DECISIONS TO PROVIDE SPECIAL HELP OR ENRICHMENT

Performance on a screening test is only one basis for the decision to make a referral for intensive assessment and consideration for special placement. Teachers also use classroom tests, daily observations, interviews, and the data they collect as part of continuous progress monitoring to decide whether a student is in need of special assistance. All of these data are part of the assessment process. Providing special assistance does not necessarily mean providing special education services. Rather, as a "first line of defense," most teachers give special help to students who experience difficulty. This help may be in the form of tutoring, a study buddy, or adaptation of classroom materials and instruction. The help may be **remedial** (designed to correct a deficit or difficulty), **compensatory** (designed to make up for a disability), or **enriching** (designed to enhance classroom activities).

REFERRAL TO AN INTERVENTION ASSISTANCE TEAM

When a student does not make satisfactory progress, even with special help, the teacher may seek assistance from an **intervention assistance team (IAT)**. This team is usually made up of general education teachers who help one another come up with ways to assist students who are having difficulties. The IAT (sometimes called a teacher assistance team, mainstream assistance team, or schoolwide assistance team) works together to solve problems. To determine whether to seek the IAT's assistance, a teacher collects information as part of routine instruction/assessment, as well as from monitoring the success of his or her own efforts to provide special help.

DECISIONS TO PROVIDE INTERVENTION ASSISTANCE

The interventions developed and put in place by intervention assistance teams are typically called **prereferral interventions** (or intervention assistance) because they occur before formal referral for child study. At the time we wrote this book, prereferral interventions were required in two-thirds of states. The prereferral intervention process has been put in place in states and local school districts in an effort to reduce referrals for testing and prevent overidentification of students for special education services. Prereferral interventions were instituted because many of the difficulties for which students were being referred could be alleviated by adjusting classroom instruction and environments. The purpose of prereferral interventions is twofold:

Alleviate learning difficulties.

Document the techniques that do and do not improve student outcomes.

For example, Pennsylvania has a special project, called the Instructional Support Team Project, to address the misclassification of students as disabled. It is designed to intervene early in students' experiences of difficulty. The members of the IST may gather data through observations, interviews, and/or tests. When they do so, they are engaging in **formal assessment**.

In efforts like the Instructional Support Team Project, team members receive formal training in assessment. The interventions suggested by these teams may involve remediation, compensation, or enrichment.

DECISIONS TO REFER FOR EVALUATION

When a student fails to make satisfactory progress, even with the help of an intervention assistance team, the student may be referred for formal psychoeducational evaluation. Referral usually is a relatively formal process involving the completion of a referral form and a formal request for a **child-study team** of professionals to decide whether a student's learning needs are sufficient to require special education services. This team is usually called a child-study team; although in some states and districts within states, these teams go by other names (e.g., IEP team or special education eligibility team). The child-study team typically includes:

General education teachers

Special education teachers

One or more administrators

The student's parent(s)

Related services personnel (school psychologist, nurse, social worker, or counselor)

Child-study teams make two basic kinds of decisions:

1. Exceptionality decisions (whether or not the child is disabled or gifted)

2. Verification of special learning needs

EXCEPTIONALITY DECISIONS

A child-study team makes exceptionality decisions when they determine whether a student meets the criteria for being declared eligible for special education services, as specified by the state in which the student lives. If, for example, the student must have an IQ (intelligence quotient) below 70 as well as deficits in adaptive behavior in order to be identified as having mental retardation, then the child-study team administers tests to see if the student meets the requirements. If the requirements are met, the team officially assigns a disability name. Teams decide whether students are blind, deaf, mentally retarded, emotionally disturbed, learning disabled, and so forth. Teams also decide whether students are gifted and talented. They are required to gather assessment information. It is illegal to base exceptionality decisions on a single test.

DECISIONS ABOUT SPECIAL LEARNING NEEDS

Child-study teams also decide whether students have special learning needs. For example, for a student who is blind, they may document that without instruction in braille, the student will experience academic difficulties. The team makes formal statements about the special learning needs of the student and the specific needs that require special education assistance. Study teams rely on the data and documentation they receive from prereferral interventions with individual students. For a more in-depth look at the process IATs use to develop prereferral interventions, see the Bringing Learning to Life sidebar, "Collaborative Intervention Planning."

Bringing Learning to Life: Collaborative Intervention Planning

The intervention assistance team (IAT) at Madison Elementary School meets regularly to develop prereferral interventions for students. The team is comprised of general classroom teachers and the special education resource teacher. They work together to develop interventions for students. In planning interventions, the team members use assessment information gained through observations, student interviews, teacher interviews, and student work. Team members go through the following steps in the collaborative planning process:

1. A teacher or teachers describe the concerns they have for the student. In doing so, they differentiate clearly between the student's actual performance and the kind of performance they want the student to demonstrate.

(Continued)

(Continued)

2. Team members share information on how instruction currently is planned, managed, delivered, and evaluated for the student. They report the results obtained using *The Functional Assessment of Academic Behavior (FAAB)* (Ysseldyke & Christenson, 2002), a system used to gather information about the student's instructional needs in the context of classroom and home environments.

3. Team members arrive at consensus about a student's instructional needs.

4. Team members then use *FAAB* to describe home support for activities taking place in the student's instructional program.

5. Team members identify ways to involve the student's parent(s) or guardian(s) and invite their assistance.

6. Team members brainstorm ideas and options for the intervention. All ideas are permitted, and their merits and limitations are not discussed.

7. The team selects appropriate intervention(s).

8. Team members share resources and discuss ways they can work together to implement the selected intervention(s).

DECISIONS ABOUT ELIGIBILITY
OR ENTITLEMENT

After the child-study team has specified a student's exceptionality and special learning needs, the team can declare the student to be *eligible* for (or *entitled* to) special education services. For the student to be eligible, the team must find *both:*

1. Exceptionality

2. Special learning needs

If these two conditions are met, the team will move on to develop an **individualized education plan (IEP)**, a process that requires decisions about instructional planning.

INSTRUCTIONAL PLANNING DECISIONS

General education teachers are able to take a standard curriculum and plan instruction around it. Although curriculums vary from district to district—largely as a function of the values of the particular community and school—they are appropriate for most students at a given age or grade level. However, when students need special help to benefit from a standard curriculum, school personnel must gather data to plan special programs.

Three kinds of decisions are made in instructional planning:

1. Deciding what to teach

2. Deciding how to teach it

3. Communicating realistic expectations

Deciding *what* to teach is a content decision, usually made on the basis of a systematic analysis of the skills that students do and do not have. Scores on tests and other information help teachers decide whether students have specific skills. Teachers also use information gathered from observations and interviews to decide what to teach.

Teachers obtain information about *how* to teach by trying a variety of methods and then monitoring students' progress toward instructional goals.

Teachers communicate realistic expectations by letting students know precisely what they are expected to do (the instructional goals) and the consequences of meeting or not meeting the goals.

PROGRESS EVALUATION DECISIONS

Teachers collect assessment information to decide whether their students are making progress. They may give unit tests, or they may have students keep portfolios of their work. They also rely on their observations of individual students' behavior, as well as their more subjective feelings and impressions of each student's work.

The best way to evaluate individual student progress is to measure whether students have mastered a sample of a large number of the skills being taught. This allows teachers to measure the extent to which students have mastered content and to chart their progress toward meeting instructional objectives.

PROGRAM EVALUATION DECISIONS

Educators collect assessment data in order to evaluate specific programs and determine how effective the curriculum is in meeting the goals and objectives of the school. School personnel typically use this information for schoolwide curriculum planning. For example, a school may compare two approaches to teaching in a content area by:

1. Giving tests at the beginning of the year

2. Teaching two comparable groups in two different ways

3. Giving tests at the end of the year

By comparing students' performances before and after, the school is able to evaluate the effectiveness of the two competing approaches.

Large-Scale Program Evaluation

The process of assessing educational programs can be complex if a large number of students is involved and if the criteria for making decisions are written in statistical terms. For example, an evaluation of two instructional programs might involve gathering data from hundreds of students and comparing their performances using statistical tests. Program costs, teacher and student opinions, and the nature of each program's goals and objectives versus those of the curriculum might be compared to determine which program is more effective. This kind of large-scale evaluation probably would be undertaken by a group of administrators working for a school district.

Teachers' Own Evaluations

Program evaluations can be much less formal. When a teacher wants to know how effective the instructional method is that she is using, she does her own evaluation. For example, recently a teacher wanted to know if having students complete activities in their basal readers was as effective as having them use language experience activities. She compared students' written products using both methods and concluded that their language experience stories were better.

ACCOUNTABILITY DECISIONS

Public schools have come under increasing criticism in the past 20 years. In 1983 the National Commission on Excellence in Education issued a report, called *A Nation at Risk: The Imperative for Educational Reform*, in which it raised concerns about education and the accomplishments of students. Increasingly, parents want reports on how students are faring at the schools to which they send their children, legislators want to know how schools are performing, and policymakers want data on the educational performance of the nation's youth. School personnel regularly administer tests to students, assess portfolios or performance, and issue reports on the achievement of the students in their schools. This information is then used to determine **accountability**—the extent to which particular schools, administrators, or teachers should be held responsible for students' performance. The No Child Left Behind Act (2001) includes the expectation that students will be assessed every year. School districts must report annually to their respective State Departments of Education, and State Departments of Education must report annually to the U.S. Department of Education on the performance and progress of all of their students.

2

What Are the Most Common Assessment Practices?

A number of terms are used to describe assessment practices. These terms sometimes change over time as new assessment practices are developed and old ones are modified. Common terms are:

Curriculum-based assessment

Curriculum-based measurement

Instructional diagnosis

Academic time analysis

Assessment of instructional environments

Outcomes-based accountability

Performance assessment

CURRICULUM-BASED ASSESSMENT

Curriculum-based assessment is "a procedure for determining the instructional needs of a student based on the student's ongoing performance within existing course content" (Gickling & Havertape, 1981, p. 55). This kind of assessment includes:

Direct observation and analysis of the learning environment

Analysis of the processes students use to approach tasks

Examination of students' products

Controlling and arranging tasks for students

General education teachers use performance on curriculum-based measures to decide which students are making satisfactory progress and which have special learning needs. Curriculum-based assessment is also used to make all the other types of decisions, from screening through accountability, listed in *Table 1.1*. See the sidebar *Point of View—The Value of Curriculum-Based Assessment* for further discussion of curriculum-based assessment.

Point of View:
The Value of Curriculum-Based Assessment

Curriculum-based assessment, when conducted properly, can be an important tool for teachers and diagnostic specialists in a number of ways.

1. Analysis of the Learning Environment

By carefully examining the learning environment, educators identify pitfalls that may be interfering with a student's learning. Such assessment can isolate problems with the instructional materials, with the ways in which instruction is organized or sequenced, with the manner of presentation (such as lecture or workbook), and with the grouping of students in the classroom.

2. Analysis of Task-Approach Strategies

By focusing on the strategies a student uses when approaching a task, teachers can identify basic learning skills that the student may need to develop.

3. Examination of Student's Products

Through systematic examination of a student's work samples, educators can spot particular error patterns.

4. Controlling and Arranging Student Tasks

By manipulating the ways in which materials are presented and the specific tasks that students are asked to perform, teachers determine which approaches are most productive.

5. An Invaluable Tool

Curriculum-based assessment is invaluable for helping teachers decide what to teach. In addition, it offers these benefits (Choate, Bennett, Enright, Miller, Poteet, & Rakes, 1987):

- It complies with the procedural requirements of the Individuals With Disabilities Education Act (Public Law 105–17) for assessing students in need of special education.
- It is efficient.
- It is a valid, reliable basis for making decisions.
- It can be used to make various kinds of decisions (e.g., screening and program effectiveness).
- It increases students' achievement.

CURRICULUM-BASED MEASUREMENT

Curriculum-based measurement (CBM) has been defined as a simple set of procedures for repeated measurement of student growth toward long-term instructional goals (Deno, 1985). Each curriculum-based measure is derived as a brief sample of all of the skills that are taught in a specific subject area at a particular grade level. These brief performance measures are administered weekly or monthly as a measure of progress toward the long-term goals. The essential purpose of CBM has always been to aide teachers in evaluating the effectiveness of the instruction they provide to individual students.

INSTRUCTIONAL DIAGNOSIS

Instructional diagnosis, another common assessment practice, is used to identify the extent to which a student's poor performance is caused by poor instruction and to indicate possible remedies for the problem. Instructional diagnosis is a systematic analysis of the requirements of instruction, including the kinds of demands put on the learner. Educators look at the skills required to complete instructional tasks and compare them to the skills a student does and does not have.

One part of instructional diagnosis is **task analysis**, the process of breaking complex tasks into their component skills. In task analysis, a complex skill, like brushing one's teeth, is broken down into its component skills (e.g., opening the toothpaste, getting out the toothbrush, applying the toothpaste, turning on the water, etc.).

ACADEMIC TIME ANALYSIS

Academic time analysis is the study of how time is allocated in school. Educators can use the computer program *Ecobehavioral Assessment System Software (EBASS)* developed by Greenwood and Carta (1993) to gather data on the exact amounts or proportions of time students spend engaged in academic work (**academic engaged time**), inappropriate behavior, and so forth. With *EBASS*, educators can report academic engaged time for individual pupils. They can also use the data as part of a systematic assessment of:

How students spend their time in school

The specific inappropriate behaviors they demonstrate

The events that trigger appropriate and inappropriate behaviors (**ecobehavioral assessment,** or the assessment of the relationship between contextual factors and student behavior)

ASSESSMENT OF INSTRUCTIONAL ENVIRONMENTS

The bottom line in assessment is improved instruction and instructional outcomes for students. As educators develop instructional interventions, they measure the extent to which the various factors lead to improved outcomes. When educators assess students' needs in the context of classroom and home environments, and when they systematically appraise the presence or absence of components of effectiveness, they are engaging in **assessment of instructional environments** (Ysseldyke & Christenson, 2002).

OUTCOMES-BASED ACCOUNTABILITY

As the demand for accountability merges with the movement toward measuring school effectiveness in terms of specific outcomes, school personnel are being asked to engage in **outcomes-based accountability**—formal assessment of the extent to which pupils are meeting designated outcomes. State education agencies are required to report annually on the performance and progress of students with disabilities.

PERFORMANCE ASSESSMENT

School personnel increasingly are assessing performance. **Performance assessment** involves gathering data on student performance directly by having them work singly or in groups to perform tasks. Data are gathered on the quality with which tasks are completed, as well as on how students work together to perform tasks.

How Are Assessment Data Collected?

Whether you teach or work with students in general or special education programs, assessment will be a large part of your daily routine. It makes sense, therefore, to know something about the methods used to gather educational information and the kinds of information those methods provide. You also will need this knowledge because federal law requires that eligibility decisions be based not on just one source of information, but on multiple sources.

METHODS FOR COLLECTING DATA

As an educator, you will use four processes to gather information about students who are exceptional:

Testing is the process of administering a set of items to obtain a score. A test is a collection of items designed to measure knowledge in a content area.

Observing is the process of watching a student perform a set of behaviors to obtain information about the rate or duration of those behaviors. An observation is a record of performance.

Interviewing is the process of asking questions to obtain information about a student's background, current levels of performance, and plans. An interview is a set of questions designed to provide information about a content area of interest.

Work sample assessment involves collecting the products of a student's work. Because these products can be put into portfolios, this method sometimes is called **portfolio assessment**.

Teachers and other professionals use tests, observations, interviews, and work samples to make decisions about students. There are no fixed rules for deciding which assessment methods to use. Educators choose the methods that provide the best information for the decision at hand. Suppose you are gathering data to decide whether a student is eligible for special education. For such a decision, most states require that an individual test of intelligence be administered, so you would use a test. To evaluate a student's ongoing progress, you might use daily or weekly observations. In making screening and referral decisions, you might use rating scales or other types of interviews.

TESTS

You've taken hundreds of tests over the years, so varied in form and content that they probably would confuse even the most able classifier. When confronted with large amounts of information, it is helpful to use categories to organize what we know. For example, grouping tests into *formal* and *informal* measures is a practical way to organize them; or we can group them by the way they are given, their format, their purpose, or their content.

Formal and Informal Measures

Formal tests have standardized administration procedures and usually are produced by test development companies. They often are designed for use with large groups of people, but some are primarily for testing individuals. Tests taken at the end of the school year during elementary, middle, and high school are good examples of formal tests.

Informal tests often are developed by teachers to measure knowledge in an area that was recently taught. Teachers assign grades in academic content areas using social studies unit tests, weekly spelling tests, and 15-item math tests, just to name a few. Because these tests vary from year to year, are usually created by the teacher before they are given, and are administered without strict adherence to standardized procedures, they are thought of as informal measures.

Group and Individual Tests

Another way to describe tests is according to the way in which they are administered. They can be **group administered** (given to an entire class at once) or **individually administered** (given to one student at a time). The primary advantage of group administration is that data can be obtained on an entire class in a relatively short time. Individual administration gives the examiner an opportunity to observe the student being tested more closely and to gather data on how the student earns his or her score.

Test Formats

Tests are also categorized according to the way the items are presented and responses are obtained. For example, on most tests, items are read to the students or the students are required to read the items themselves. Some tests require written responses in multiple-choice form; others require short answers or essays. Students give verbal answers on some tests; on others, they "perform" their answers, by choosing one item from several items, by putting puzzles together, or by performing some other physical action.

Screening and Diagnostics

Tests also differ in their intended uses. **Screening tests** are used to spot students who are making too little or too much progress, compared either to others or to the objectives of the curriculum. **Diagnostic tests** provide more specific information, usually in the form of a description of strengths and weaknesses in the development of a specific skill.

Norm- and Criterion-Referenced Tests

Tests also are either norm referenced or criterion referenced; these terms describe the way in which test results are used, more than the actual format of the test. When norm-referenced interpretations are made, the student's performance is compared to the performance of other students.

Norm-referenced tests are standardized at the time they are developed; that is, they are given to a large number of students to obtain an index of "typical" or "average" performance. An individual's performance on the test is compared to that of a national or local sample of students of the same age or grade level. By definition, students who earn significantly higher or lower scores than their agemates or grademates are said to perform abnormally. Students who perform very poorly on a test relative to others their age are said to be deficient in the area of performance; those who do much better than their agemates are said to be exceptionally proficient.

Criterion-referenced tests give teachers a measure of the extent to which individuals or groups have mastered specific curriculum content. These tests also are called objective-referenced tests or curriculum-based tests, names that reflect what the tests are designed to do. These tests are developed by specifying the objectives or criteria to be mastered, usually in basic skill areas like reading and mathematics, then writing items to assess mastery of objectives or criteria. The results indicate the degree to which the content or skill representing a particular instructional objective has been mastered; they are used to describe what each student has learned and needs to learn in a specific content area.

Test Content

We also can describe tests according to the content of the items. In special education, tests commonly are used to assess intelligence, achievement, sensory acuity, perceptual-motor abilities, adaptive behavior, language functioning, and personality development. Scores on these and other measures can be found in the school records of virtually every student who receives special education services.

OBSERVATIONS

Observations vary in the way information is collected. **Active observations** record ongoing behavior. When a teacher sits beside a student and watches her do math problems, he is using active observation. He also uses active observation when he records the amount of time the student is out of her seat or the number of times she raises her hand to ask for help.

When a teacher looks at the product a student produced last week, at test records, or at information in a student's cumulative folder, she is using **passive observation**.

Another way to describe observations is in terms of the action or product being observed. Classroom behaviors, academic tasks, vocational skills, interpersonal skills, and athletic performance are examples of actions or products observed in school settings. Like tests, observations also can be **formal** (using systematic procedures) or **informal** (using spontaneous data collection procedures).

Teachers, other school professionals, and parents make observations as part of the educational process to gather the information needed to make decisions. Observations provide different information than that available from tests and interviews. They are used when information is not available from other assessment sources or to verify information collected from those other sources. For example, in gathering data on a student's activity level we could ask the teacher to rate level of activity, or we could interview teachers or parents and ask them to describe a student's activity level. We could also observe the student's behavior. We use our observations to confirm and support information gathered from other sources (e.g., rating scales, interviews).

INTERVIEWS

An **interview** (asking questions to obtain information about a person's background, current levels of performance, and future plans) is a popular method of gathering assessment information. Interviews are conducted to obtain information from a group or from one person about a student, or they are conducted with the student directly. For example, at the beginning of the school year, a teacher may ask parents and the students themselves to complete a survey about attitudes toward school. The teacher compares the responses of the parents with those of the respective students, and then uses the information to decide how to motivate and teach each student.

Educators most often describe interviews in terms of form. Like tests and observations, interviews can be **formal** (predetermined, written down, and administered the same way each time) or **informal** (developed as the interview proceeds from initial questions). They also can be structured or unstructured. In a **structured interview**, the interviewer asks the same set of questions in the same way each time. In an **unstructured interview**, the exact nature of the interview is not known before it is administered. The interviewer asks a question, and then, depending on the student's answer, the interviewer asks another question related to it. In all interviews, students respond orally or in writing.

Interviews can touch on any topic, from name, address, and phone number to opinions about parents and pets. One teacher asks each of his students the following questions during the first days of the school year:

1. What is your favorite subject in school?

2. What is your least favorite subject in school?

3. When some students complete a project, they still want to work on it to make it better. How about you?

4. When some students receive a low grade, they try to improve it. How about you?

5. Some students try different ways to solve problems before giving up. How about you?

6. Some students really like school. How about you?

The information from this brief survey is used to make decisions about which students to put together for group projects. It also helps the teacher get to know his students a little better early in the school year.

WORK PORTFOLIOS

Many teachers now have their students make **work portfolios** (extensive collections of the products of students' work). Besides reviewing individual products to see if students are performing tasks correctly, they review entire portfolios to make judgments about the extent to which students are making progress. As efforts are made to move away from using multiple-choice tests to make decisions about students, more teachers are being asked to keep portfolios of students' work. State education agencies in some states (e.g., Kentucky and Minnesota) have developed **rubrics** (rules and procedures for scoring) for evaluating portfolios.

4

Which Methods of Assessment Should Be Used to Sample Certain Behaviors and Abilities?

Any test, observation, interview, or work portfolio is just a sampling of the items that can be used to assess an ability, skill, or characteristic. For example, there are literally hundreds of items that can be used to assess the math achievement of fifth graders. A test contains only a sample of items. An observation is a sample of a student's behavior. Obviously, educators can't watch everything a student does at all times during the school day; in an observation they must select what is to be observed and when to observe it. In the same way, the questions in an interview are just a sample of those that could be asked. Remember this when you are collecting and evaluating information about students: *What you collect is a sample of behavior, and the way you collect it controls the answers you get.*

The behaviors most often sampled by assessment are:

Intellectual abilities

Academic achievement

Sensory acuity

Adaptive behavior

Language development

Psychological development

Perceptual-motor development

INTELLECTUAL ABILITIES

Intellectual abilities are generally assessed by intelligence tests, formal and informal observations, and interviews.

Testing Intelligence

School personnel regularly use intelligence tests to identify the extent to which students demonstrate thinking and problem-solving skills. They look for **discrepant scores**, scores that are significantly lower or higher than the norm. Students who demonstrate lower levels of intelligence are thought to learn more slowly than their agemates; those who demonstrate higher levels of intelligence are thought to learn more quickly than their agemates. Both types of students are a challenge for general education classroom teachers. They do not fit easily into the organization, goals, and activities of the typical classroom.

Many intelligence tests sample behaviors. Authors develop tests that sample the specific behaviors they think best reflect the performance being measured. *Table 4.1* lists 13 kinds of behaviors sampled by intelligence tests.

Observing Intelligence

Observations are used to assess intellectual abilities. For example, as part of a psychoeducational evaluation, a teacher might be asked to record the number of four types of questions that a student asks during reading over a week's time. The teacher might also be asked to supply previously written products as evidence of a student's higher levels of thinking.

Table 4.1   Kinds of Behavior Sampled by Intelligence Tests

Nature of Task	Performance Required
Discrimination	Given a set of stimuli, the student is required to find the one that differs from all the others. The stimuli may be figures, symbols, or words.
Generalization	Given a stimulus, the student must select from among a number of response alternatives the one that is most like the stimulus. Both the stimulus and response alternatives may be figures, symbols, or words.
Sequencing	Given a series, the student must identify the one that comes next in the series.
Analogies	The student must respond to an item of an A: B: C: ? nature. The student must identify a relationship between A and B, then identify from several alternatives the one that has the same relationship to C as A does to B.
Motor behavior	The student may be required to walk, place geometric forms in a recessed form board, copy geometric designs, trace paths through a maze, and so on.
General information	The student is required to answer specific factual questions.
Vocabulary	The student is required to define words or to point to pictures that illustrate words read by the examiner.
Induction	The student is presented with a series of examples and required to induce a governing principle.
Comprehension	The student must give evidence of understanding directions, printed material, or societal customs and mores.

(Continued)

Table 4.1 (Continued)

Nature of Task	Performance Required
Detail recognition	Students are judged on the extent to which they recognize details in drawing pictures, find hidden objects in pictures, or recall details of a story.
Abstract reasoning	Students are required to state the meaning of proverbs, solve arithmetic story problems, and so on.
Memory	Several kinds of tasks are used to assess student skill in remembering items, objects, details of stories, sequences of digits, and so on.
Pattern completion	Given a pattern, students must select from among response items the one that completes the pattern.

Informal observations gathered during the administration of a test can be revealing. For example, when asked general information questions on an intelligence test, one student consistently gave expansive answers. When asked which European first encountered America, the student answered: "Some people say Christopher Columbus, some say Amerigo Vespucci, some people say Leif Erickson; actually, nobody really knows." When asked the sum of two numbers, the student supplied the answer and gave five more number sentences like it. When the testing was over, the school psychologist commented that the student was the smartest she had ever tested. Her opinion was based not only on the student's score on the test, but also on informal observations of the student's performance.

Intelligence Interviews

Interviews are another source of information about a student's intellectual abilities. Many school districts use screening checklists to identify students who may need special education enrichment or acceleration. These rating scales usually are administered to parents or teachers, and contain items like these:

Use the following scale (1 = strongly disagree, 2 = disagree, 3 = unsure, 4 = agree, 5 = strongly agree) to indicate the extent to which you agree with each of the following statements.

This student (My child) . . .	1	2	3	4	5
1. demonstrates superior thinking abilities.					
2. demonstrates excellent memory for details.					
3. demonstrates creative problem-solving skills.					

ACADEMIC ACHIEVEMENT

It was mentioned earlier that students, teachers, and parents need to know if progress is being made in academic subject areas of instruction. Achievement tests often are used to provide this information. There are literally hundreds of published achievement tests.

Achievement Tests

Achievement tests measure skill development in academic content areas. Some measure skill development in multiple content areas (e.g., math and reading); others concentrate on one content area (e.g., spelling). The *Metropolitan Achievement Tests* (Harcourt Educational Measurement, 2001) are an example of group-administered, norm- or criterion-referenced screening tests. They assess skill development in several content areas. The *Gray Oral Reading Test–4* (Wiederholt & Bryant, 2001) is an individually administered, norm-referenced diagnostic measure that provides specific information on skill development in oral reading.

Observations of Achievement

Teachers use **observations** gathered while tests are being administered to help them understand a student's performance. They also use analyses of permanent products. For example, two students may earn exactly the same score on a mathematics achievement test, but demonstrate very different math skills on more detailed analysis of their written products. Consider the test performances of Bob and Jim. Each performed nine items correctly on a math test. Both their scores may be represented as 60 percent correct or 40 percent incorrect. Similarly, if Bob and Jim are the same age, the number of correct items may be converted to age-equivalent scores, grade-equivalent scores, percentiles, quotients, standard scores, or other derived scores that are exactly the same.

However, even though Bob and Jim receive the same score, Bob's performance on the test is different from Jim's. Using **error analysis**, systematic analysis of the kinds of errors a student makes, we can see, for example, that Bob has mastered multiplication; Jim has not. This kind of analysis provides more data for making decisions about a student's academic abilities.

Observations also can be valuable in deciding what to teach. For example, by observing how students read, teachers can uncover the errors students make and identify the factors that may be limiting their reading performance. Ekwall (1981) describes over 20 types of errors that students often make in reading and recommends ways to correct them. By recognizing and correcting specific types of reading errors, teachers are more likely to see improvement in reading scores than if they simply ask students to read without regard to the quality of the effort.

Achievement Interviews

Teachers use **informal interviews** to gain insight into factors that influence their students' performances. They may ask students for their opinions about the work in the textbook and their preferences for doing workbook assignments, teacher-made worksheets, or homework. They may also ask questions designed to assess their fears of particular subjects such as math. In this case, a teacher may use the last questions in an interview to estimate students' mastery of number facts, computation, problem solving, fractions, and other mathematics skills.

Other teachers may use informal interviews to gain insight into the factors that facilitate or inhibit students' performance in reading. Students' answers may indicate that they are bored by basal reading activities, are confused by new words, or prefer to read silently. Some teachers ask students to rank their word recognition skills when reading in science, social studies, health, and other content areas. Students may also be asked to rank the ways they remember words (sounding them out, using word parts, using meanings). By recording students' responses to questions about their learning patterns and reading methods, teachers know what has been effective in the past.

Achievement and Portfolios

Portfolio assessment usually consists of collecting samples of students' work—their writing samples, drawings, poems, samples of their mathematics problem-solving, and so forth. Portfolios may also include CDs or videos of student performances. A collection of products that demonstrate what a student has accomplished and, by inference, is capable of doing, a **portfolio** is defined formally as

> a purposeful, interrelated collection of student work that exhibits the student's efforts, progress, and achievement in one or more areas. The collection includes student participation in selecting contents, the criteria for selection, the criteria for judging merit, and evidence of student self reflection. The portfolio communicates what is learned and why it is important. (Paulson, Paulson, & Meyer, 1991, p. 60)

SENSORY ACUITY

Poor academic performance is sometimes caused by problems with seeing and hearing. Although severe sensory impairments are almost always diagnosed before a child begins school, tests of visual and auditory acuity are used regularly in assessments of students who are having difficulties in school.

Testing Vision and Hearing

The simplest test of visual acuity uses the Snellen Wall Chart. The student being tested stands 20 feet away from the chart and tries to read it. An adaptation of the Snellen Chart, the Snellen E, is used to assess preschool students and those who are unable to read.

An **audiometer** is used to assess hearing acuity. A pure-tone audiometer generates pure tones at varying frequencies and at varying degrees of loudness.

Observations of Sensory Acuity

Teachers also make informal assessments of sensory acuity by watching how students read and how they act when asked questions, and by asking them about how they approach tasks. Teachers watch their students and ask themselves questions:

Can students see the chalkboard from their seats, or do they need to be closer to it to see or hear better?

Do they tilt their heads or squint when reading from textbooks and other printed materials?

Do they complain about itchy eyes or squint when focusing on objects?

Do their visual skills differ in the classroom from on the playground or in other areas of school?

Do they often ask for directions to be repeated?

Teachers often interview students with special learning needs. They also ask parents to complete questionnaires about the students' visual and auditory abilities as a way of learning more about how to help students succeed in school. A section of an interview form is shown in *Figure 4.1.*

Figure 4.1   Sample Questions from an Interview Form

Visual Abilities

1. Does your child require any special considerations relative to the use of vision in the classroom? If yes, what are they?

2. Does your child have trouble reading from the chalkboard? If yes, what helps?

3. Does your child require special reading materials (for example, large-print books)? If yes, what are they and do you have access to them?

4. Does your child wear glasses or use a magnifying glass or other visual aids?

Auditory Abilities

Does your child require any special considerations relative to the use of hearing in the classroom? If yes, what are they?

Does your child use alternative communication systems (e.g., sign language, lip reading)? If yes, which one(s)?

Does your child require special adaptations from speakers (slower pace, alterations of loudness)? If yes, what are they?

Does your child wear a hearing aid? If yes, is there anything special that I should know about it?

ADAPTIVE BEHAVIOR

There was a time when students were classified as mentally retarded on the sole basis of their performance on an intelligence test. In 1969, a report from the President's Committee on Mental Retardation indicated that many students classified as mentally retarded actually demonstrated normal behaviors outside of school. The phrase "six-hour retarded child" was coined to describe students who had been labeled mentally retarded in school but who were functioning normally out of school, in other environments. Because so much of performance on intelligence tests is based on general knowledge gained in school, it was reasoned that additional criteria should be used in the decision to classify a student as mentally retarded.

In 1973, the American Association on Mental Deficiency (AAMD) modified its definition of mental retardation to include both subaverage intellectual functioning and deficits in adaptive behavior. It defined **adaptive behavior** as "the effectiveness or degree with which the individual meets the standards of personal independence and social responsibility expected of his age and social group" (Grossman, 1983, p. 11). That definition was "legitimized" with the enactment of the Education for All Handicapped Children Act (Public Law 94–142) in 1975 and reaffirmed with the passage of the Individuals With Disabilities Act (IDEA) in 1990.

Adaptive Behavior Scales

Adaptive behavior scales are not tests per se. They use interviews with parents, teachers, or others familiar with the student to assess his or her behavior. For example, many adaptive behavior scales provide information about the student's **self-help skills** (e.g., eating, dressing, toileting), **communication skills** (e.g., imitating sounds, following directions), and **occupational and social skills** (e.g., using money, doing chores, playing games). A common measure of adaptive behavior is provided by the American Association on Mental Deficiency (AAMD).

Environments and Adaptive Behavior

Assessing adaptive behavior is not an easy process. To evaluate the extent to which someone's behavior is adaptive, or normal, in an environment, we must first identify the environment and understand the behaviors that are socially acceptable in that environment.

There are two frames of reference for deciding whether a behavior is conforming:

1. Is it deemed acceptable by most people, by a majority or public culture?

2. Is it deemed acceptable by a few people, by a minority or private culture?

Behaviors may be adaptive, or conforming, in the majority or public culture, and nonadaptive in a minority culture, or vice versa. For example, some adolescents dress in ways considered adaptive in their "goth" culture, while others dress in ways not adaptive to that culture. For this reason, it is difficult to develop a standardized measure of adaptive behavior. People's tolerance for particular behaviors depends on the type of behavior, the context in which it is exhibited, the status of the individual exhibiting the behavior, and the orientation (and presence) of the observer.

LANGUAGE DEVELOPMENT

For many students, poor academic performance is a function of immature or deficient language development. Language development can be assessed using tests, observations, and interviews.

Tests of Language

Tests exist for all levels of language development and functioning. They measure four components of language:

Phonology

Morphology

Syntax

Semantics

Tests that are designed specifically to assess aspects of language require the student to provide language samples, which are then evaluated. Some tests also evaluate comprehension, with items that require the student to follow simple directions or to imitate words, phrases, and sentences. Language functioning also is a part of other tests, especially tests of intelligence and academic achievement.

Observations of Language

Teachers assess the language development of their students through formal and informal observations. They may count the number of specific classes of speech problems (e.g., part-word repetitions and whole-word repetitions) under a variety of conditions (reading, conversation), or they may assess fluency by counting syllables or words produced during a timed speech sample. Teachers may also keep track of articulation errors (e.g., "wabbit" for rabbit), distortions ("bulu" for blue), and omissions ("pay" for play). Some teachers use video, audio, or written transcriptions to study their students' speech.

Language Interviews

Background information about a student's language development generally is collected from parents using a structured-interview approach. A good interview does more than ask questions like "Does your child talk?" or "When did your child start to talk?"; it addresses how the child uses language. For example, a speech therapist may interview parents using a form that contains questions like these:

1. Is speech easy to understand?

2. Is speech pleasant to hear?

3. Is speech linguistically appropriate?

4. Is speech labored in production?

5. Are content and manner of speech appropriate?

In assessing language development, usually a background interview comes first. Next, observations of the components of language development are completed as a basis for understanding how a student uses language in natural settings. Finally, standardized tests are used to provide information on selected aspects of language ability and to provide corroborative evidence for the strengths and weaknesses identified through other methods of assessment. In addition, portfolios could be used to assess language development.

Psychological Development

Psychological development is assessed by having students draw family pictures or self-portraits, answer open-ended questions about themselves, or respond to ambiguous pictures, drawings, or situations. These responses are evaluated for evidence of clinical or diagnostic pathology (e.g., excessive fear of death, aggressiveness, or inadequacy).

Personality Tests

The use of personality tests in schools has diminished over the years. But in some schools, these tests are used extensively and may even be required to classify students as having emotional disturbance. In some districts, school psychologists conduct personality tests; in others, professionals in private practice are contracted by the school to assess students' psychological development.

Psychological Observations

Observations play an important part in the assessment of psychological development because inappropriate behavior is seen as an indicator of abnormal development. Any action can be the target of a formal or informal observation. The procedure is straightforward. First, the class of problem behavior to be observed is described in terms that can be counted. For example, the category of inappropriate behavior might include counts for not sitting in an assigned seat, looking out the window instead of at an assignment, talking without permission, and not completing assignments. Next, a system for measuring each target behavior is selected and applied. Finally, the counts are tallied and reported. Counts can be recorded in various ways:

• **Interval recording** measures the number of time blocks in which a behavior or response occurs. For example, the teacher divides an observation period (say, ten minutes) into smaller intervals (say, 30 seconds) and checks whether the behavior being monitored occurs at any time during an interval.

• **Time sample recording** measures the number of times a behavior or response occurs after a preset interval (e.g., ten seconds or two minutes). When using time samples, a teacher sets an interval period (such as every two minutes), then checks at the end of the interval and records whether the target behavior is occurring at that time.

• **Event recording** measures the number of times a behavior or response occurs during a preset observation period. For example, a teacher counts the number of times a student raises her hand during a 30-minute observation period.

• **Duration recording** measures the length of time over which a behavior or response occurs. When teachers use this method, they record the time a behavior starts and stops. Then they calculate the cumulative total time (e.g., 48 minutes) for the observation period (such as 60 minutes) as a record of how long the behavior occurred.

• **Latency recording** measures the time between a request for behavior and an actual response. When teachers use this method, they record the time they ask a student to perform a behavior and the time the student starts doing it.

Psychological Interviews

Teachers' and parents' ratings are used extensively in assessing students who are thought to have emotional problems. These interviews vary considerably in form and content. For example, some require yes or no answers to questions about specific behaviors exhibited by the student being evaluated. Others use a Likert-type response format (1 = strongly agree . . . 5 = strongly disagree) to indicate the extent to which an item reflects the problems of the student being assessed. Most of the scales contain several dimensions of problem behaviors. The *Revised Behavior Problem Checklist* contains six problem behaviors: conduct disorders, socialized aggression, attention problems/immaturity, anxiety/withdrawal, psychotic behavior, and motor excesses (Quay, 1983). The *Walker Problem Behavior Identification Checklist* contains five (Walker, 1983):

Acting out: The student complains about discrimination or unfairness and becomes upset when things don't go the way he or she would like.

Withdrawal: The student has few friends, does not initiate interpersonal interactions, and does not engage in group activities.

Distractibility: The student is restless, continually moves, seeks attention more than other students, and easily loses interest in tasks and learning activities.

Disturbed peer relations: The student makes negative self-statements and comments that nobody likes him or her.

Immaturity: The student reacts to stress with physical complaints (stomach hurts, headaches) and cries easily.

PERCEPTUAL-MOTOR DEVELOPMENT

Many educators believe that being able to translate sensory information into meaningful actions is important for success in school. For example, some special educators argue that a student who cannot copy a geometric design (e.g., a square or diamond) will have difficulty copying letters and numbers when working on academic tasks.

Perceptual-Motor Tests

Tests of perceptual-motor development require students to copy designs or perform other actions after being told or shown what to do.

The *Bender Visual Motor Gestalt Test* (Koppitz, 1963; Brannigan & Decker, 2003) is a good example of a perceptual-motor assessment device. It consists of nine geometric shapes that the student is asked to copy on a plain sheet of white paper. The reproductions are scored relative to four types of errors:

Shape distortions

Perseveration

Integration

Rotation

Errors are scored as **shape distortions** when a student's design is distorted to the extent that a representation of the original figure is lost. **Perseveration** errors are scored when a student fails to stop after completing the required picture. **Integration** errors result when parts of a design overlap or fail to meet. **Rotation** errors are scored when a student shifts a design more than 45 degrees from the way it was presented.

Perceptual-Motor Observations

Educators use observations to assess students' perceptual-motor development. On the playground a teacher may keep track of the way a student walks, skips, and runs around, as well as the student's catching and throwing skills. When the student is working on art projects, the teacher watches how well he or she colors within the lines and uses scissors.

Perceptual-Motor Interviews

Many teachers also ask parents, other teachers, and students themselves about perceptual-motor skills. Students who lack these skills often are assigned to training programs. This practice is common with students who have learning disabilities, mental retardation, physical impairments, or have multiple disabilities.

5

What Standards Must Be Met to Ensure the Accuracy of an Assessment?

In addition to understanding the kinds of behaviors sampled by tests, observations, interviews, and student portfolios, and the ways in which assessment data are used, you should understand the three technical aspects of assessment practices:

Reliability

Representativeness of performance

Validity

RELIABILITY: IS PERFORMANCE CONSISTENT?

Tests, observations, interviews, and collections of student work samples should provide consistent measures of performance. This means that different examiners, each using the same procedures with a specific student, should be able to obtain comparable results, and that the student should earn comparable scores on repeated administrations. Inconsistent performance sometimes reflects a student's responses to the various examiners or illness during one of the testing sessions, not simply a problem with the test itself. But the value of a measure is very much a product of its reliability.

Reliability is an index of consistency in measurement. Test, observation, interview, and work-sample scores that fluctuate considerably on repeated measurement, either by different examiners over time or by separate administrations of the same measure, may not be reliable. Authors are supposed to include information in their technical manuals on the reliability of their instruments. Reliability is expressed as a **coefficient**, an index of the degree of relationship between scores earned on two administrations of a test. Reliability coefficients range from .00 to .99.

How high should reliability be? It depends on how you are using the scores. Two standards of reliability generally are accepted for use in educational decision making:

> **Group data**: When scores are being used for general purposes and are reported for groups, they should have a reliability of at least .60.

> **Individual data:** When scores are used to make placement decisions about individual students, the minimum standard is .90. When a referral decision is being made, .80 is the accepted standard.

REPRESENTATIVENESS: DOES THE INSTRUMENT ADEQUATELY SAMPLE THE BEHAVIOR?

An assessment instrument should include adequate samples of the behavior being tested. The more extensively an instrument samples the behavior, the better it is. Tests, observations, interviews, and portfolios cannot sample all aspects of a behavior, but they must sample enough to be **representative**. At the same time, procedures must be manageable in terms of time and costs.

Representativeness also has to do with item content. To be technically adequate, an assessment instrument must sample the appropriate kinds of behaviors. This means math tests should include math items and reading tests should include reading items. It also means that observations should include different types of acceptable actions (e.g., sitting in an assigned seat, maintaining eye contact when talking to another person, raising a hand before asking or answering a question). Further, it means that rating scales of adaptive behavior must contain more than a few items about independent living skills.

VALIDITY: DOES A PROCEDURE MEASURE WHAT IT IS SUPPOSED TO MEASURE?

Suppose a colleague developed a test to measure her students' skills in volleyball. If you wanted to use her test, how would you know whether it measured what she said it measured? It is the author's responsibility to provide evidence of the test's validity. **Validity** can be demonstrated in many ways, for example:

Performance on a measure of word recognition is shown to be highly related to performance on other measures of word recognition. Students who do well on one test of reading do well on other reading tests, or they simply read well.

People who earn high scores on a test of mechanical aptitude and who choose to become mechanics are shown to become successful mechanics; those who earn low scores do not.

Successful typists are shown to earn high scores on a measure of typing speed; less proficient typists earn lower scores.

People who have the best understanding of the content of this book earn the highest scores on a measure of understanding the content of this book.

Window on Practice—Developing a Test

Would you like to develop a test that could be published and then used by others? In most areas of human endeavor, whether art or technology, the product appears deceptively simple to accomplish. This is often the case with test development. If you try it, you may find the work arduous, but you can also find it interesting and stimulating.

Most professional test developers have had advanced training in a special branch of statistics called **measurement theory**. Your task of developing a test is facilitated not only by special training but also by the presence of certain character traits: Since your task requires attention to detail over a long period of time, it helps to become a compulsive neurotic. It also helps to develop a taste for delayed gratification, for the fruits of your labor may not be seen for years. Finally, you should strive to become a bit sadistic, a trait especially helpful when you must test young children for hours in order to gather important data.

Of course, you must have an idea for a test. Opportunities do exist. In the field of special education there are many potential areas of measurement for which no one has developed a good test. Your test might be the one that will help others. What would you like to measure? An aspect of school achievement? Adaptive behavior? Cognitive ability? Perhaps motivation or attention?

After you identify the area, other decisions remain. Is your test to be a clinical procedure administered to one subject at a time, or a group test that can be administered to an entire classroom? With which age range is the test to be used? Is the interpretation of an examinee's performance to be norm referenced (compared to peers) or criterion referenced (compared to curriculum objectives)?

Given the prerequisite personality characteristics for test development and an idea, what is next? The steps followed in test development are fairly standard and, in a sense, a form of engineering. First, the test design and specifications are prepared. Several more questions must be answered. How are the test questions to be presented (orally, read by the examinee, by pantomime)? What kinds of responses do you want from the examinees (written, oral, pointing)? What kinds of derived scores will the users of your test need (grade equivalents, age equivalents, standard scores, percentile ranks)?

Once you have designed the test, you must prepare a pool of potential test items, usually at least twice as many as you expect to use in the final form of the test. (You'll be surprised how many of your favorite items prove inadequate once they are given a trial.) Keep in mind that your item pool is only a sampling of the knowledge or skills you want to measure; therefore, you must carefully analyze the area to be measured and then prepare a pool of items that represents a good cross-section.

Now conduct a series of small-scale tryouts, initially with only a small group of subjects. These tryouts allow you to polish the test administration procedures, improve item content and wording, and detect potential scoring problems. One outcome of this step is likely to be the realization that you need to develop even more items. Another possible outcome is you notice that you do not have enough easy items, or perhaps you decide you should measure one aspect in your test more thoroughly.

After this revision step, it is time to repeat the process of evaluating and editing your fledgling test again. This cycle will be repeated three or four times before you are satisfied that you have created a good draft of your test. Then you are ready to begin the process of standardizing the test.

Two goals are involved in standardizing a norm-referenced test. First, the test is administered under controlled, documented conditions that will be followed by subsequent test users.

The second goal is to obtain normative data, which allow future users to compare the scores they obtain to the scores obtained by the subjects in your norming sample. The user of a standardized test usually wants to compare a person's performance on a test to the performance of others at the same age or grade placement. The people

(Continued)

(Continued)

included in your norming sample must be carefully selected so that they provide a good cross-section of the population to which your test users want to compare their scores. This requires careful attention to factors such as a geographic distribution of your sample and personal characteristics such as race, sex, and socioeconomic variables. Finally, the test items are arranged in the final form from the easiest to the most difficult. The data from your norming study tell you that sequence.

Your users will expect you to provide information about the reliability and validity of your test. The reliability information tells how precisely your test measures. The validity information tells how well your test measures what it is intended to measure.

Your last step is to prepare the testing materials, including the manuals your users need. This step makes all your efforts useful to others. The better you complete this part of your project, the easier it is for others to use your test in the way you intended.

And that's about all there is to it. That is, until it is time to revise your test.

Source: Richard W. Woodcock is an educational consultant and developer of the Woodcock-Johnson Psychoeducational Battery–Revised and the Woodcock Reading Mastery Tests–Revised.

Observations made during atypical or insufficient time periods by untrained or biased people of unrepresentative behaviors are not valid measures of a student's performance. Similarly, interviews conducted by people with little knowledge of the student being evaluated or by people with biased opinions are not appropriate sources of information for making decisions.

6

What Concerns Do Parents, Students, and the General Public Have About Assessments?

Those who develop tests and who administer and interpret them worry about the technical factors of reliability, representativeness, and validity. The general public does not typically think or talk about technical concepts like reliability, representativeness, and validity. Rather, they worry about test fairness, acceptability, and consequences. In this section we illustrate how the concerns of the lay public parallel those of test developers and users.

TEST FAIRNESS

We've all heard people talk about tests that were fair or unfair. Fairness is a fuzzy concept and a marker for a varied set of grievances. For example, when some people call tests unfair, they are arguing that the test is used to make unfair comparisons. You may have heard one of your friends make statements like "It is unfair to compare me to shorter people" or "It is unfair to compare me to younger people." Some argue that tests are unfair when they include measures of things the test takers have not had an opportunity to learn. Others use the concept of fairness in discussions of **haloed** or **stereotypic judgments**, judgments in which the decision maker is influenced more by a stereotype held for the student's race, gender, ethnicity, or background than by the student's actual performance and behavior.

Concerns about fairness also include those raised by students about content coverage of tests. You may have taken a test you thought was unfair: one in which the content tested was not, in your opinion, representative of the content covered in a class. This concern also includes objections raised by students who are tested on content they thought they would not be tested on (e.g., the professor said the test would cover only the lecture content, but it included content from the book).

Test developers go to great lengths to ensure that their tests are not viewed as unfair. They do so by trying to use representative groups for purposes of comparisons and by trying to be sure that tests are valid and accurate measures.

ACCEPTABILITY

Sometimes people argue that it is not fair to test them and to make judgments about them. Individuals who consider themselves professionals (including teachers) sometimes contend that they should not be tested or evaluated. They believe they, not others, should make judgments about their performance. In short, they find evaluation or testing unacceptable.

Arguments about acceptability include the contention that testing is undemocratic and elitist. Some argue, for example, that colleges and universities should not use tests to make decisions about who gets into undergraduate or graduate programs. They contend that testing is not "authentic" and that all people should be admitted. Those who use tests to make selection or admission decisions contend that they do not have resources to admit everyone and that tests help them identify those for whom admission is appropriate.

Many of the concerns people raise about acceptability are based on their judgments about face validity. **Face validity** refers to the extent to which a test looks fair. Of course, judgments about whether a test looks fair are just that: judgments. They are influenced very much by personal biases and beliefs.

Sometimes parents contend that testing their children is unacceptable. This contention may be an ethnic or religious contention—the argument that "_____ children should never be tested." This argument is often expressed by parents of students with disabilities. They make statements like "It is cruel to subject my child to this kind of testing experience."

CONSEQUENCES

The general public worries about the consequences of testing, such as using tests to decide who graduates from school, who gets a job, who gets into college, who gets certified or licensed, and who gets a driver's license. Those who develop and use tests translate such concerns into concerns about accuracy and generalizability. They try to develop measures that provide accurate information that generalizes from one setting to another.

7

What Are the Assumptions Underlying Assessment Practices?

Assessment is the basis on which professionals decide who should receive special education services, where and by whom those services will be delivered, the specific nature of instructional treatments, and the criteria used in evaluating the effectiveness of those treatments. In reaching their decisions, educators make basic assumptions about assessment procedures. In order to understand the use of assessment—and its possible misuse—you need to understand four assumptions:

The examiner is skilled.

Future behavior can be inferred from present behavior.

Assessment is relatively free from error.

Students have comparable acculturation.

THE EXAMINER IS SKILLED

When students are assessed, it is assumed that the person doing the assessment is trained to establish rapport with the students and knows how to administer, score, and interpret the instrument used to collect the assessment information. To the extent that rapport is not adequately established and the instrument is administered, scored, and interpreted incorrectly, the results are not valid.

Establishing Rapport

Establishing **rapport** means making the student feel comfortable in the test situation and motivated to do his or her best. Suppose you wanted to remove Pat from a third-grade classroom to give him a reading test. It probably wouldn't be a good idea to enter the classroom and shout "Next victim." You certainly wouldn't march Pat down the hall to the testing room and say "Read." Instead you would talk to him about hobbies or TV programs or some other interest. Once you entered the testing room, you might have Pat draw pictures or tell a story to relax. Your task is to make the student feel comfortable. There are no rules for that; different techniques work with different students. However, remember that your main purpose is to test the student. Some examiners spend so much time getting the student ready for testing that when they get to the test itself, the student has lost interest.

Training to Administer Tests

An examiner must know how to administer an instrument. Obviously if an instrument is not administered correctly, the student's performance has little meaning. The amount and type of needed training vary with the type of assessment and its purpose. Special training is needed to administer, score, and interpret most individually administered tests. For many group tests, just reading the test manual is enough. Similarly, some observation instruments require formal training, while others can be completed simply by counting target behaviors. Very few interviews require extensive training, but most commercially available rating scales provide administration guidelines in their technical manuals. The gathering of portfolios of student work requires only that the teacher or student collect the work.

Scoring

The examiner must be able to score the assessment instrument. In this age of electronic scoring, teachers seldom have to worry about scoring group-administered intelligence and achievement tests, although they should check electronic scoring when the results are suspect (e.g., a gifted student's scores are below average, or the best reader in the class performs poorly). Most individually administered tests are scored by the examiner. All tests should include information about scoring in the test manual. Extra care should be taken when compiling scores on observations. Inaccurate counts of observed behaviors can result in misinterpretation of the extent of a student's skills or problems.

Interpreting Results

Finally, the examiner must know how to interpret the student's performance. For some procedures this means simply reporting the student's scores. For others, it means learning how to interpret the score.

FUTURE BEHAVIOR CAN BE INFERRED FROM PRESENT BEHAVIOR

The second assumption underlying any assessment is that future behavior can be inferred from the present behavior that is being measured. We have said that all tests, observations, interviews, and portfolios are samples of behavior. If we were trying to predict performance on the assembly line in an automobile plant, for example, the best assessment would be to watch the individual working on the assembly line. In most instances, however, this isn't possible, so we would sample the target behavior in different ways. We'd choose a form of assessment that we believed would predict future performance. To predict performance on an assembly line, we could not use a spelling test, but we could use a manual-dexterity test. Future behavior can never be observed, so any prediction about future behavior is an **inference**. Inferences have different degrees of plausibility, depending on the similarity between the behavior sampled and the behavior being predicted.

ASSESSMENT IS RELATIVELY FREE FROM ERROR

People who rely on assessment instruments tend to assume they are accurate. But educational, psychological, and behavioral tests, observations, work samples, and interviews are not perfect measures of skills, characteristics, or abilities.

On any day, a student can make a careless mistake on a test or assignment, or an answer may simply be a guess. The student's scores are inaccurate to the extent that careless mistakes are made and some answers are guesses. The scores that students earn on tests always are made up of two components: true score and error. To the extent that error is present, the score is inaccurate.

In observations and interviews, we also must be concerned about the extent of error present in scores. After a teacher observes a student, she asks herself if the performance she recorded is typical of the student's behavior. Brown (1981) describes four types of common errors in rating scales:

1. **Errors of central tendency:** Raters tend to avoid extreme points on a continuum, overusing the middle categories.

2. **Errors of leniency:** Raters often are generous in their ratings.

3. **Severity errors:** Raters also can be too stringent in their ratings.

4. **Halo effect errors:** Raters sometimes allow their general impressions and opinions to influence their ratings.

5. **Logical errors:** Raters sometimes assume characteristics or behaviors are related when they are not.

Obviously, what people say about another person does not always reflect what the person does. When using observations or interviews, try to be aware of your own attitudes and preconceptions that may influence the process. Special care is needed with interviews because the respondent is the sole source of the information.

STUDENTS HAVE COMPARABLE ACCULTURATION

Acculturation refers to the way a person's background experiences and opportunities shape his or her acquisition of the society's culture. The fourth major assumption in assessment is that the student has comparable, not necessarily identical, acculturation to those with whom he or she is being compared; that is, that the student being assessed has had experiences and opportunities similar to those in the norm group.

According to standards specified by a joint committee of the American Psychological Association, the American Educational Research Association, and the National Council on Measurement in Education (1999), the manuals that accompany assessments must tell users the precise nature of the group on whom the instrument was standardized. Sufficient information should be provided on the age, gender, grade level, socioeconomic status, and geographic region of the norm group so that others can judge the extent to which the student being assessed is like the norm group. To the extent that students differ from the norm group, judgments based on comparisons are invalid.

What Guidelines Should Be Followed for Appropriate Assessment?

Assessment is central to special education because students cannot receive special services or leave special programs without it. Assessment also is the basis of planning, implementation, and evaluation decisions. Given the importance of assessment in the lives of exceptional students, you should know something about "best practices." The following eight guidelines provide a foundation for proper assessment:

1. There is no one way to do it right.

2. There is no one cause of school problems.

3. Assessment must do more than describe problems.

4. Assessment should be directed at improving instruction.

5. Assessment should occur often during teaching.

6. Assessment should concentrate on relevant variables.

7. Assessment should occur where the behavior occurs.

8. Tests should be adapted to accommodate students with disabilities.

There Is No One Way to Do It Right

There is no recipe for assessment—no single battery of tests, form of observation, specific rating scale, or portfolio of student work that can tell us everything we want to know about any student. Remember that assessment is the process of collecting data for the purpose of making decisions about students. Only if all students had the same kinds of problems could there be one right way to assess them. Assessment activities must be tailored to the individual and to the nature of the instructional setting.

There Is No One Cause of School Problems

One of the major failings of assessment practices is that many of those practices are driven by a "search for pathology." Students with academic and behavioral problems are assessed because somebody thinks there's something wrong with them. Sometimes there is; students do have sensory, communication, physical, emotional, and intellectual difficulties that are significant enough to interfere with learning. Those problems may be so evident that assessors can assume they are the primary problem.

But often the problems students experience in school have to do with instruction and the goals or demands of the school. Problems occur in a context: home, classroom, or home-school relationships or interactions. Assessors need to operate from a broad perspective, looking beyond the student to take into account the context in which difficulties arise.

Assessment Must Do More Than Describe Problems

Sometimes school personnel spend far too much time searching for and describing students' problems. They gather extensive information, develop elaborate profiles, and write lengthy descriptions of students' dysfunctions, defects, deficits, and disabilities. Then they share these descriptions with parents, colleagues, and school administrators. This process seldom benefits students. It is our job to solve problems and develop students' competencies. Unless assessment practices facilitate the development of competence, they are of limited value.

Bringing Learning to Life: The Hypothetical Word Processing Test

Suppose you are the personnel manager of a large industrial firm that does business around the world. Part of your job involves hiring word processors. You regularly require applicants to take a word processing test, which includes typing from handwritten English and from dictation. You score the test for both speed and accuracy. Sounds pretty simple, doesn't it? You expect the test to provide representative, valid results that will help you decide whom to hire.

But even if you give each applicant the same test, you need some basis for evaluating the performance. So you have to standardize your test, that is, you develop a set of norms according to which applicants' performances can be evaluated. There are many groups on which such a test could be standardized; for example, any of the following:

1. All high school seniors in your local school district

2. All high school seniors in your local school district who have been enrolled in a business curriculum

(Continued)

(Continued)

and who have taken at least one full year of word processing classes

3. A representative national sample of high school seniors who have been enrolled in a business curriculum and who have taken at least one full year of word processing classes

4. All the people who, over a three-year period, have applied for employment with your company

5. All the people who, over a three-year period, have applied for employment as word processors with your company

6. Persons currently employed as word processors in your company who have better than satisfactory performance evaluations from their immediate supervisors

The nature of the group you select for standardizing the test will influence your judgment of individual applicants. An applicant might look very good compared with high school seniors but poor compared with currently employed, successful word processors.

Consider what will happen to an excellent typist who has never worked from a dictation device. Such a person might do very well on the typing-from-handwriting portion of the test but not as well on the part that includes dictation. If your norm group consisted of experienced word processors, that person's overall score might not meet your standards.

Consider the fate of an applicant who recently immigrated to the United States from China. This applicant, whose spoken English is excellent, types very fast but makes several spelling errors on both portions of the test. (Your test, remember, is in English.) If your norm group included few new immigrants, this applicant might be eliminated, even if your company does extensive business in China and needs more word processors who can type both English and Chinese.

If such problems can occur with a simple word processing test, imagine the difficulties with the complex, multidimensional instruments used in educational assessment. That is why tests are supposed to include detailed information about the norm group on which they were standardized. If a student's acculturation differs substantially from that of the norm group, the test is not a valid basis for comparison.

ASSESSMENT MUST BE DIRECTED AT IMPROVING INSTRUCTION

The ultimate goal of assessment is to identify problems with instruction and to lead to instructional modifications. Many present-day assessment activities consist of little more than meddling. Many professionals gather data simply because they find those data interesting, which isn't enough. We must use assessment data to improve instruction.

ASSESSMENT SHOULD OCCUR OFTEN DURING TEACHING

Effective teachers frequently assess students and programs. It is impossible to be sure about the best ways to teach students, so teachers choose an approach (their best guess), then measure the extent to which progress is made. The only way to determine the effectiveness of instruction is to collect data.

Assessment Should Concentrate on Relevant Variables

For whatever reasons, much of current assessment is irrelevant to instructional decision making. Diagnostic personnel regularly administer intelligence tests, achievement tests, and other tests without thinking about the reasons for testing students. They conduct comprehensive interviews that bear little relation to the problems they are trying to solve. These practices are inappropriate and unnecessary. We don't always need information on cognitive functioning, general achievement, or personality functioning to improve instruction for students who are failing in school.

The most relevant variable to look at when students have problems is the extent to which teaching is occurring. When students fail to read adequately, it may be because they have had little instruction in reading. Large numbers of students may fail to do well in mathematics because they seldom practice working with numbers. Although it is often important to assess the learner and the nature of instruction, the way to begin any assessment is by evaluating the extent to which:

1. Instruction has occurred.

2. The student has played an active part in learning.

Many teachers and school psychologists think they must look at literally every area of functioning to uncover a student's problem. They are wrong. Assessment should be directed toward identifying factors that can improve instruction. The classroom is clearly the place to start.

Assessment Should Occur Where the Behavior Occurs

To the extent possible, data on student performance should be collected in the environment where that performance occurs. If a student's performance in mathematics is of concern, math performance should be assessed in the classroom where it is a problem, with the materials the student uses. This approach allows much less room for inference than does assessment outside the classroom using a math test not related to the curriculum.

One of the authors of this textbook was once a school psychologist and, having been trained to do so, often tested students. As was common practice in those days, he would remove students from the classroom and then administer a number of reading tests. Later, when he would describe a student's "reading" to the classroom teacher, more often than not he would be told that the measure overestimated or underestimated the student's actual ability. Students perform differently in different settings with different people; the best place to assess performance is in the environment where a behavior occurs.

TESTS SHOULD BE ADAPTED TO ACCOMMODATE STUDENTS

Major efforts are underway to include students with disabilities in all assessments without biasing the results against them (Ysseldyke & Thurlow, 1993). To accomplish this goal, modifications must be made in tests or in testing procedures in order to provide a more accurate picture of students' accomplishments. Some of the most important test modifications are:

Flexible scheduling: Tests can be administered during several brief sessions rather than a single lengthy one.

Flexible setting: Students can be allowed to take tests in a separate room with fewer or no people present rather than in a large auditorium.

Alternatives for recording answers: Students with disabilities may be allowed to record their answers directly in a test booklet rather than filling in electronically scored answer sheets.

Alternative-print format: Students with visual disabilities can be given tests in large-print or braille versions.

9

Assessment in Perspective

M any teachers have been taught that it is their job to spot students who are having difficulty and that they or someone else ought to spend time and effort identifying deficits or disabilities. Often they don't know what they are looking for, but the search itself is exciting. Currently a kind of test mania exists in many schools. Parents and teachers worry about overlooking students' problems. They worry that a problem left uncovered may irreparably damage a student. We don't agree. Serious problems become obvious early, usually well before a child begins school. The real danger is not in overlooking a problem but in identifying a disorder where one does not exist.

ASSESSMENT IN THE CLASSROOM

Assessment is an ongoing part of the special education process. Assessment data are used to determine eligibility, the special education program, and the effectiveness of that program. The best place to collect assessment data is in the classroom, and we encourage you to make regular use of tests, observations, interviews, and student portfolios when you teach. We also encourage you to use the information you gather as a record of students' present levels of functioning, not primarily as an indicator of underlying problems.

THE EFFECTS OF ASSESSMENT

Assessment is a process of collecting data for the purpose of making decisions about students. This book describes the kinds of decisions that are made. Many of the decisions have a significant effect on students' life opportunities. Therefore, assessment is an activity that must be taken very seriously.

10

What Have We Learned?

As you complete your study of effective assessment for students with special needs, it may be helpful to review what you have learned. To help you check your understanding, we have listed the key points and key vocabulary for you to review. We have included the Self-Assessment again so you can compare what you know now with what you knew as you began your study. Finally, we provide a few topics for you to think about and some activities for you to do "on your own."

KEY POINTS

▣ Assessment is the collection of information about a student for the purpose of making decisions. Assessment information is used to make the following kinds of decisions: screening, provision of special help, referral to an intervention assistance team (IAT), provision of intervention assistance, referral to a child-study team, exceptionality, presence of special learning needs, eligibility or entitlement for special education, instructional planning, progress evaluation, program evaluation, and accountability decisions.

▣ For students to be considered eligible for special education services, child-study teams must demonstrate that the students meet the eligibility criteria for the conditions of special education as specified in their state, and that they have special learning needs that require special education assistance.

▣ Tests, observations, interviews, and portfolios are methods used to gather assessment information across a range of behaviors, skills, abilities, and characteristics. The information collected in the assessment process is just a sample, and it is controlled by the way in which it is collected.

▣ Both lay people and assessors have concerns about assessment and the assessment process. Lay people tend to be concerned about fairness, acceptability, and consequences. Assessors tend to be concerned about reliability, representativeness, and validity.

▣ A set of fundamental assumptions underlies current assessment practices; when those assumptions are violated, the results of the assessment are invalid.

▣ Guidelines for appropriate assessment include the following: Assessment must do more than describe problems, should be directed at improving instruction, should occur often during teaching, should concentrate on relevant variables, and should occur where the behavior occurs.

▣ Assessment practices are changing and being improved frequently, and it is wise to monitor these changes.

Key Vocabulary

Academic engaged time is the exact amount or proportion of time students spend engaged in academic work.

Academic time analysis is a systematic observation and recording of time students are engaged in responding to academic instruction.

Accommodations are changes in testing materials or procedures that enable students to participate in assessments in ways that reflect their skills and abilities rather than their disabilities.

Accountability decisions consist of using scores on tests to hold individuals, schools, teachers, districts, or states responsible for student educational results.

Acculturation refers to a student's particular set of background experiences and opportunities to learn in both formal and informal educational settings.

Achievement test measures a student's skill development in academic content areas.

Active observation is a record of ongoing behavior.

Adaptive behavior is behavior that meets the standards of personal independence and social responsibility expected of an individual's age and cultural group.

Assessment is the process of collecting data to make decisions about students.

Assessment of instructional environments occurs when educators assess students' needs in the context of classroom and home environments, and when they systematically appraise the presence or absence of the components of effectiveness.

Audiometer is used to assess hearing acuity.

Child-study team is a group that determines a student's eligibility for special education and develops an individualized education plan (IEP); typically composed of teachers, other representatives of the school district, and the child's parents.

Compensatory education is instruction that teaches a student to compensate for a disability; an example is teaching braille.

Criterion-referenced tests are tests in which the individual's performance is interpreted relative to specific curricular objectives that have been mastered; evaluates a pupil's absolute level of mastery. Also called *objective-referenced test* and *curriculum-based test*.

Curriculum-based assessment is a procedure for determining the instructional needs of a student on the basis of the student's ongoing performance in a content area.

Curriculum-based measurement is a simple set of procedures for repeated measurement of student growth toward long-term instructional goals.

Diagnostic tests provide specific information about a student, usually in the form of a description of strengths and weaknesses in the development of a specific skill.

Discrepant scores are scores that are significantly lower or higher than the norm.

Duration recording measures the length of time over which a behavior or response occurs.

Ecobehavioral assessment is the assessment of the relationship between contextual factors and student behavior.

Eligibility decision is the specification of a student's exceptionality and special learning needs, and the subsequent decision of whether or not to provide the student with special education.

Enrichment is the enhancement of the educational experiences of students with materials or activities that go beyond the standard curriculum; does not involve changing students' placement or educational setting.

Error analysis is the systematic analysis of the kinds of errors a student makes.

Event recording measures the number of times a behavior or response occurs during a preset observation period.

Exceptionality decisions are the specifications of a student's exceptionality and special learning needs, and the subsequent decisions of whether or not to provide the student with special education.

Face validity refers to the extent to which a test looks fair.

Formal tests have standardized administration procedures and usually are produced by test development companies.

Group-administered tests are given to an entire class at once.

Individually administered tests are given to one student at a time.

Individualized education plan (IEP) is a written document that includes (1) a statement of the student's present levels of functioning, (2) a statement of annual goals and short-term objectives for achieving those goals, (3) a statement of services to be provided and the extent of regular programming, (4) the start date and expected duration of services, and (5) evaluation procedures and criteria for monitoring progress.

Inference is any prediction about future behavior.

Informal interview is an interview in which questions develop as the interview proceeds from initial questions; used to gain insight into factors that influence student performance.

Informal tests often are developed by teachers to measure knowledge in an area that was recently taught; they are administered without strict adherence to standardized procedures.

Instructional diagnosis is an effort to identify the extent to which a student's poor performance is caused by poor instruction and to determine possible remedies.

Interval recording measures the number of time blocks in which a behavior or response occurs.

Intervention assistance team (IAT) is a school-based group designed to help teachers solve problems with individual students.

Interviewing is asking questions to obtain information about an individual's background, current levels of performance, and plans.

Latency recording measures the time between a request for behavior and an actual response.

Norm-referenced test is a standardized test in which the performance of the individual is compared to that of others who are of the same age or grade level.

Norms are cutoff scores to help educators make decisions; the scores are based on the performance of those who took the test during development.

Observation is a record created through the process of watching a student perform a set of behaviors.

Passive observation is a record created from looking at a student's products or test records or at information in the student's cumulative folder.

Perceptual-motor tests are tests of the ability to translate sensory information into meaningful actions; they require students to copy designs or perform other actions after being told or shown what to do.

Performance assessment involves gathering data on student performance directly by having them work singly or in groups to perform tasks.

Prereferral intervention includes finding ways to improve a student's functioning in the regular classroom without referring the student for special education.

Portfolio is a collection of products of an individual's work.

Portfolio assessment is the process of assessing a collection of products of an individual's work; sometimes called *work-sample assessment.*

Program evaluation decision is made when educators collect assessment data in order to evaluate specific programs and determine how effective the curriculum is at meeting the goals and objectives of the school.

Progress evaluation decision is the determination as to whether or not students are making progress.

Psychoeducational assessment consists of individually administered psychological and educational tests.

Reliability is an index of consistency in measurement; the extent to which results of the measurement can be generalized to different observers and times.

Reliability coefficient is an index of the degree of relationship between scores earned on two administrations of a test; ranges from .00 to .99.

Remedial education is instruction designed to repair or correct deficits in performance by training students in deficit areas.

Representativeness is the extent to which an assessment instrument adequately samples the behavior being measured.

Screening is the collection of data to determine whether more intensive assessment is necessary.

Stereotypic judgments are judgments in which the decision maker is influenced more by a stereotype held for the student's race, gender, ethnicity, or background than by the student's actual performance and behavior.

Task analysis is the breaking down of complex behaviors or skills into their component parts or subskills.

Testing is the administering of a set of items to obtain a score.

Time sampling recording measures the number of times a behavior or response occurs after a preset interval.

Validity is the extent to which a test measures what it claims to measure.

Work-sample assessment is the process of assessing a collection of products of an individual's work; sometimes called *portfolio assessment*.

Self-Assessment 2

After you complete this book, check your knowledge and understanding of the content covered. Choose the best answer for each of the following questions.

1. _____ is not a way to gather data on students.

    a. Record review

    b. Observation

    c. Interviewing

    d. Revelation

2. The process of collecting data to decide whether more intensive assessment is needed is called:

    a. Referral

    b. Screening

    c. Program evaluation

    d. Eligibility determination

3. The process of breaking complex student work into component skills is called:

    a. Task analysis

    b. Portfolio assessment

    c. Ecobehavioral assessment

    d. Performance assessment

4. When one assesses those skills necessary to perform successfully in a setting (e.g., college) we call this:

   a. Portfolio assessment

   b. Environmental appraisal

   c. Job analysis

   d. Inference

5. Scores that are significantly above or below average are called:

   a. Scaled scores

   b. Normal curve equivalents

   c. Discrepant scores

   d. Percentiles

6. Tests that measure skills in academic content areas are called:

   a. Content assessments

   b. Achievement tests

   c. Diagnostic tests

   d. Personality tests

7. _____ is the measurement term used to refer to consistency in measurement.

   a. Validity

   b. Reliability

   c. Representativeness

   d. Correlation

8. Assessment is:

   a. Testing students to determine their strengths and weaknesses

   b. A process of collecting data for the purpose of making decisions

   c. Always tailored to the individual

   d. Testing used to decide who is eligible for special education

9. When a test is modified to provide a more appropriate picture of a person with a specific disability, this is called:

   a. Accommodation

   b. Flexibility

   c. Accountability

   d. Alternate assessment

10. Which is true?

    a. Assessment is a way to test.

    b. Assessment should be directed at improving instruction.

    c. Students who perform poorly on tests are eligible for special education services.

    d. Students who are disadvantaged perform poorly on tests.

REFLECTION

1. Throughout this book we have referred to formal and informal assessment procedures and to structured and unstructured procedures. For example, we talked about informal assessment, structured interviews, unstructured

interviews, and formal assessment. Distinguish between formal and informal approaches, and between structured and unstructured approaches.

2. Identify four kinds of behaviors sampled by intelligence tests, and say how they are different.

3. We identified several assumptions about the skills of those who give tests. Name four. What is the effect of violating the assumptions?

4. *Acculturation* is a term used to describe an individual's background of experiences and knowledge. Why is it important that those who assess students take acculturation into account? How does acculturation affect test performance? What happens if an examiner fails to consider a student's acculturation when making assessment decisions?

Answer Key for Self-Assessments

1. d

2. b

3. a

4. b

5. c

6. b

7. b

8. b

9. a

10. b

On Your Own

☑ Obtain any commercial test. Write down five test items, and then state the kind of behavior each samples.

☑ List five kinds of behaviors that could be sampled in an assessment of intelligence.

☑ Develop a scrapbook on assessment practices by collecting articles on assessment from local newspapers and magazines. For each of the articles you collect, indicate the kind of decision-making activity in which assessment information is being used (e.g., to make accountability decisions).

☑ Visit an elementary school classroom. Pick any student at random and observe the student for an hour or two. Keep a tally of the number of 20-second intervals in which the student is:
– Actively engaged in responding to academic materials
– Doing something else

☑ Write a summary of your observations.

☑ Visit a local elementary school classroom. Pick a student at random and observe the student for two hours. During that time, record the amount of time that:
– The teacher shows or tells the student what to do
– The student spends demonstrating that he or she understands what is being taught
– The student is tested on mastery of what has been taught

☑ Write a summary of your observations.

Resources

BOOKS

Impara, J. C., & Plake, B. S. (Eds.). (2001). *The fourteenth mental measurements yearbook.* Lincoln: University of Nebraska Press. This yearbook critically reviews the technical adequacy of commonly used tests. This is another source to consult before selecting and using specific tests.

Maddox, T. (Ed.). (2002). *Tests: A comprehensive reference for assessments in psychology, education, and business* (5th ed.). Austin, TX: Pro-Ed. This text reviews the most commonly used educational and psychological tests. It is useful to those who are trying to decide which of several tests to use in a domain.

Salvia, J., & Ysseldyke, J. E. (2004). *Assessment* (9th ed.). Boston: Houghton Mifflin. This comprehensive textbook on psychological and educational assessment focuses on issues and concerns in assessment of students with disabilities. The text includes basic information about testing and measurement, and extensive description of assessment practices in classrooms and out of classrooms. Most of the tests commonly used with students with disabilities are described and critically evaluated.

Sattler, J. (2001). *Assessment of children: Cognitive applications* (4th ed.) and Sattler, J. (2001). *Assessment of children: Behavioral and clinical applications* (5th ed.). San Diego, CA: Author. *www.sattlerpublisher.com*. These two textbooks, written primarily for psychologists, include excellent descriptions of the use of major intellectual batteries as well as the latest research findings on specific devices and practices.

Ysseldyke, J. E., Algozzine, B., & Thurlow, M. L. (2000). *Critical issues in special education* (3rd ed.). Boston: Houghton Mifflin. Chapter 7 describes the major issues in assessment of students with disabilities. Topics include using tests to classify and place students, the use and misuse of intelligence tests, and the push for a national achievement test.

JOURNALS AND ARTICLES

Assessment for Effective Intervention. Council for Exceptional Children (CEC), 1110 North Glebe Road, Suite 300, Arlington, VA 22201. *www.cec.sped.org/* This is the official journal of the Council for Educational Diagnostic Services, the Division of the Council for Exceptional Children. It focuses on services to those who have diagnostic roles in school systems and includes critical evaluations of specific tests, comparative studies of the "goodness" of competing tests in evaluating students with disabilities, and reviews of testing advances.

Journal of Educational Measurement. NCME, 1230 17th St. NW, Washington, DC 20036. *www.ncme.org*. This is the official journal of the National Council on Measurement in Education. It is a highly technical journal. Articles deal with the psychometric characteristics of tests. The journal also publishes critical reviews of tests.

Journal of Psychoeducational Assessment. Editor, Bruce Bracken, School of Education, The College of William and Mary, Williamsburg, VA 23187–8795, or Editor, R. Steve McCallum, Department of Educational Psychology, 434 Claxton Addition,

University of Tennessee-Knoxville, TN 37996–3400. *www.psychoeducational.com*. The journal focuses on tests and research conducted on tests. It is typical to find articles on the technical adequacy (reliability and validity) of a specific test, the use of tests to make decisions about students, and testing issues.

ORGANIZATIONS

Council for Educational Diagnostic Services (CEDS)

This official division of the Council for Exceptional Children (CEC) includes school diagnosticians, resource teachers, assessment specialists, school psychologists, and others whose professional employment involves assessment of students who are exceptional. Council for Educational Diagnostic Services, Division of the Council for Exceptional Children, 1100 North Glebe Road, Suite 300, Arlington, VA 22201–5704. *www.unr.edu/educ/ceds*.

National Council on Measurement in Education (NCME)

This council includes university and test publishers, as well as educational measurement specialists and educators interested in measurement of human abilities, personality characteristics, and educational achievement. The NCME publishes two quarterlies: *Educational Measurement: Issues and Practices* and the *Journal of Educational Measurement*. NCME, 1230 17th St. NW, Washington, DC 20036. *www.ncme.org*.

References

American Psychological Association, American Educational Research Association, & National Council on Measurement in Education. (1999). *Standards for educational and psychological tests.* Washington, DC: American Educational Research Association.

Brannigan, G., & Decker, S. (2003). *Bender visual motor Gestalt test* (2nd ed.). Itasca, IC: Riverside.

Brown, F. (1981). *Measuring classroom achievement.* New York: Holt, Rinehart & Winston.

Choate, J., Bennett, T., Enright, B., Miller, L., Poteet, J., & Rakes, T. (1987). *Assessing and programming basic curriculum skills.* Boston: Allyn & Bacon.

Choate, J. S., Enright, B. E., Miller, L. J., Poteet, J. A., & Rakes, T. A. (1994). *Curriculum-based assessment and programming* (3rd ed.). Boston, MA: Allyn & Bacon.

Deno, S. L. (1985). Curriculum-based measurement: The emerging alternative. *Exceptional Children, 52,* 219–232.

Education for All Handicapped Children Act, Pub. L. N. 94–142, 89 Stat. 773 (1975).

Ekwall, E. (1981). *Locating and correcting reading difficulties* (3rd ed.). Columbus, OH: Merrill.

Gickling, E., & Havertape, J. (1981). Curriculum-based assessment. In J. Tucker (Ed.), *Non-test-based assessment.* Minneapolis: University of Minnesota, National School Psychology Inservice Training Network.

Greenwood, C., & Carta, J. (1993). *Ecobehavioral assessment system software.* Kansas City, KS: Juniper Gardens Children's Center.

Grossman, H. (Ed.). (1983). *Manual on terminology and classification in mental retardation* (Rev. ed.). Washington, DC: American Association on Mental Deficiency.

Harcourt Educational Measurement. (2001). *Metropolitan achievement tests* (8th ed.). San Antonio, TX: Author.

Individuals With Disabilities Education Act, Pub. L. No. 101–476, 104 Stat. 1141 (1990).

Individuals With Disabilities Education Act, Pub. L. No. 105–17, 111 Stat. 37 (1997).

Koppitz, E. M. (1963). *The Bender Gestalt test for young children.* New York: Grune & Stratton.

National Commission on Excellence in Education. (1983). *A nation at risk: The imperative for educational reform.* Washington, DC: Author.

No Child Left Behind Act, Pub. L. No. 107–110, 115 Stat. 1425 (2001).

Paulson, F., Paulson, P., & Meyer, C. (1991). What makes a portfolio a portfolio? *Educational Leadership, 48*(5), 60–64.

Quay, H. (1983). *Manual for the Revised Behavior Problem Checklist.* Coral Gables, FL: University of Miami.

Quay, H. C., & Peterson, D. R. (1996). *Revised Behavior Problem Checklist: Professional Manual* (PAR ed.) (RBPC). Odessa, FL: Psychological Assessment Resources.

Shanker, J. L., & Ekwall, E. F. (2002). *Locating and correcting reading difficulties* (8th ed.). Upper Saddle River, NJ: Prentice Hall.

Taylor, R. L. (2002). *Assessment of exceptional individuals* (6th ed.). Boston: Allyn & Bacon.

Walker, H. M. (1983). *Walker Problem Behavior Identification Checklist.* Los Angeles: Western Psychological Services.

Wiederholt, L., & Bryant, B. (2001). *Gray Oral Reading Test–4.* Austin, TX: Pro-Ed.

Ysseldyke, J. E., & Christenson, S. L. (2002). *The Functional Assessment of Academic Behavior (FAAB).* Longmont, CO: Sopris West Educational Services.

Ysseldyke, J. E., & Thurlow, M. L. (1993). *A self-study guide to the development of educational outcomes and indicators.* Minneapolis, MN: National Center on Educational Outcomes.

Index

Note: Numbers in **Bold** followed by a colon [:] denote the book number within which the page numbers are found.

Living arrangements, for adults with special needs
    alternative living unit, **5**:31
    foster homes, **5**:31–32
    group homes, **5**:30–31
    independent living, **5**:32
    institutions, **5**:33
Lloyd, J., **4**:40
Logical errors, **3**:62
Long, E., **12**:67
Lora v. New York City Board of Education, **2**:40 (tab)–41 (tab)
Loudness, **7**:19–20, **7**:60
Louisiana Department of Education, **13**:12
Low vision, **7**:60–61
Luckner, J., **7**:24, **7**:38, **7**:42, **7**:50
Luetke-Stahlman, B., **7**:24, **7**:42, **7**:50
Lynch, E. W., **8**:56–58, **8**:57 (tab)

Mainstreaming, **2**:54, **2**:56, **5**:29–30, **5**:56
    See also Least restrictive environment
Mangrum, C. II, **5**:26
Manifestation determination, **2**:29, **2**:56
Manual movements, **7**:40, **7**:61
Marburger, C. L., **5**:42 (tab)
Marder, C., **5**:24
Marland, S., **13**:41–42
Maryland State Department of Education, **13**:11
Mastery, defining, **9**:32
Mathematics, improving, **6**:27, **9**:32–33, **9**:34 (fig)
McBurnett, K., **9**:44
McKinney, J. D., **9**:51
McMeniman, M. M., **4**:5
Measures of process disorders, **9**:18–19

Medical disabilities, **8**:9–16
    AIDS, **8**:12–13
    cystic fibrosis, **8**:12
    fetal alcohol syndrome, **8**:14
    heart conditions, **8**:12
    hemophilia, **8**:13–14
    identification by medical symptoms, **8**:9–10
    maternal cocaine use, **8**:14–15
    medically fragile/technology dependent groups, **8**:15–16
    other health impairments, **8**:10–11 (tab)
    prevalence of, **8**:10
    special health problems, **8**:14–15
Medical procedures, to ensure appropriate education, **2**:46, **2**:48, **2**:54
Medical treatment, for emotional disturbance, **11**:37–38
Medically fragile, **8**:15, **8**:64
Medical/physical/multiple disabilities
    academic characteristics of, **8**:38
    behavioral characteristics of, **8**:39–40
    cognitive characteristics of, **8**:37–38
    communication characteristics of, **8**:40–41
    distribution of child with, **8**:7–8 (fig)
    home *vs.* institutional care for, **8**:55–56
    inclusion of student with, **8**:56
    inclusion of student with, overcoming barriers to, **8**:56–59, **8**:57 (tab)
    medical disabilities, **8**:9–16, **8**:10–11 (tab)
    multiple disabilities, **8**:33–35

Reading, improving
  analytical programs for,
    9:27, **9**:56
  fostering motivation/interest,
    9:30–32
  reading comprehension,
    9:28–30
  sight word recognition, **9**:28
  taped texts for, **9**:6
  whole language programs for,
    9:27, **9**:57
Reading Excellence Act, **6**:20
Reading First, **2**:30–31, **6**:10, **6**:20
Reality therapy, **4**:43, **4**:65
Reber, M., **8**:30
Receptive language, **10**:44
Redl, F., **4**:44
Referral, **1**:22, **1**:42
  See also Prereferral
    interventions
Reflection
  assessment, **3**:3–4, **3**:85–87
  communication disorders,
    10:5, **10**:51
  effective instruction, **4**:4, **4**:70
  emotional disturbance, **11**:3–4,
    11:51–52
  families/community agencies,
    5:3–4, **5**:59–60
  fundamentals of special
    education, **1**:4, **1**:48
  gifted and talented child,
    13:3–4, **13**:57–58
  learning disabilities,
    9:3–4, **9**:62
  legal foundations of special
    education, **2**:4, **2**:60
  medical/physical/multiple
    disabilities, **8**:3, **8**:69–70
  mental retardation, **12**:3–4,
    12:75–76
  public policy/school reform,
    6:3, **6**:49
  sensory disabilities, **7**:3, **7**:65

Regular education initiative
  (REI), **6**:21, **6**:45
Rehabilitation Act, **2**:53, **9**:44
Reichert, E. S., **13**:45
Reis, S. M., **13**:45
Related services,
  1:26, **5**:12, **10**:42
  as part of individualized
    education program,
    1:23, **11**:45, **12**:33
  defining, **1**:42–43, **6**:45
  growth in numbers receiving,
    1:19–20
  mandated, **1**:31, **2**:48, **6**:40,
    8:17, **8**:43, **12**:9
Related services personnel,
  1:20, **3**:12
Reliability, **3**:50, **3**:81
Reliability coefficient,
  3:50, **3**:81
Remedial education, **3**:10, **3**:81
Renzulli, J., **13**:18, **13**:43
Representativeness, **3**:50–51, **3**:81
Residual functioning,
  8:52–53, **8**:65
Resources
  assessment, **3**:91–93
  communication disorders,
    10:57–59
  effective instruction, **4**:75–77
  emotional disturbance,
    11:57–65
  families/community agencies,
    5:65–68
  fundamentals of special
    education, **1**:53–55
  gifted and talented child,
    13:63–65
  learning disabilities, **9**:67
  legal foundations of special
    education, **2**:65–66
  medical/physical/multiple
    disabilities, **8**:75–83
  mental retardation, **12**:81–87

**CORWIN
PRESS**

The Corwin Press logo—a raven striding across an open book—represents the union of courage and learning. Corwin Press is committed to improving education for all learners by publishing books and other professional development resources for those serving the field of PreK–12 education. By providing practical, hands-on materials, Corwin Press continues to carry out the promise of its motto: **"Helping Educators Do Their Work Better."**